GLOBALVIEWPOINTS

Famine

Other Books of Related Interest:

At Issue Series
Genetically Modified Food

Current Controversies Series
Conserving the Environment
Developing Nations
Food
Global Warming
Pollution

Introducing Issues with Opposing Viewpoints Series
Genetically Modified Food
Water Resource Management

Issues on Trial
Pollution

Opposing Viewpoints Series
Africa
Ecoarchitecture
Endangered Oceans
Poverty

GLOBALVIEWPOINTS

Famine

Diane Andrews Henningfeld, Book Editor

GREENHAVEN PRESS
A part of Gale, Cengage Learning

GALE
CENGAGE Learning

Detroit • New York • San Francisco • New Haven, Conn • Waterville, Maine • London

Christine Nasso, *Publisher*
Elizabeth Des Chenes, *Managing Editor*

For more information, contact:
Greenhaven Press
27500 Drake Rd.
Farmington Hills, MI 48331-3535
Or you can visit our Internet site at gale.cengage.com

For product information and technology assistance, contact us at

Gale Customer Support, 1-800-877-4253
For permission to use material from this text or product, submit all requests online at www.cengage.com/permissions

Further permissions questions can be emailed to permissionrequest@cengage.com

Articles in Greenhaven Press anthologies are often edited for length to meet page requirements. In addition, original titles of these works are changed to clearly present the main thesis and to explicitly indicate the author's opinion. Every effort is made to ensure that Greenhaven Press accurately reflects the original intent of the authors. Every effort has been made to trace the owners of copyrighted material.

Cover image Roberto Schmidt/AFP/Getty Images.

LIBRARY OF CONGRESS CATALOGING-IN-PUBLICATION DATA

Famine / Diane Andrews Henningfeld, book editor.
     p. cm. -- (Global viewpoints)
     Includes bibliographical references and index.
     ISBN 978-0-7377-4332-6 (hardcover)
     ISBN 978-0-7377-4331-9 (pbk.)
     1. Famines--Juvenile literature. 2. Natural disasters--Juvenile literature. 3. Nature--Effect of human beings on--Juvenile literature. 4. World politics--Juvenile literature. I. Henningfeld, Diane Andrews.
     HV630.F36 2009
     363.8--dc22

                                                                   2008055448

Printed in the United States of America
   2 3 4 5 6   13 12 11 10 09

ED363

Contents

Chapter 2: Famine and Natural Disasters

Chapter 3: Famine, Politics, and the World Economy

Foreword

"The problems of all of humanity can only be solved by all of humanity."
—Swiss author Friedrich Dürrenmatt

Global interdependence has become an undeniable reality. Mass media and technology have increased worldwide access to information and created a society of global citizens. Understanding and navigating this global community is a challenge, requiring a high degree of information literacy and a new level of learning sophistication.

Building on the success of its flagship series, *Opposing Viewpoints*, Greenhaven Press has created the *Global Viewpoints* series to examine a broad range of current, often controversial topics of worldwide importance from a variety of international perspectives. Providing students and other readers with the information they need to explore global connections and think critically about worldwide implications, each *Global Viewpoints* volume offers a panoramic view of a topic of widespread significance.

Drugs, famine, immigration—a broad, international treatment is essential to do justice to social, environmental, health, and political issues such as these. Junior high, high school, and early college students, as well as general readers, can all use *Global Viewpoints* anthologies to discern the complexities relating to each issue. Readers will be able to examine unique national perspectives while, at the same time, appreciating the interconnectedness that global priorities bring to all nations and cultures.

Material in each volume is selected from a diverse range of sources, including journals, magazines, newspapers, nonfiction books, speeches, government documents, pamphlets, organization newsletters, and position papers. *Global Viewpoints* is truly global, with material drawn primarily from international sources available in English and secondarily from U.S. sources with extensive international coverage.

Features of each volume in the *Global Viewpoints* series include:

- An **annotated table of contents** that provides a brief summary of each essay in the volume, including the name of the country or area covered in the essay.

- An **introduction** specific to the volume topic.

- A **world map** to help readers locate the countries or areas covered in the essays.

- For each viewpoint, an **introduction** that contains notes about the author and source of the viewpoint explains why material from the specific country is being presented, summarizes the main points of the viewpoint, and offers three **guided reading questions** to aid in understanding and comprehension.

- **For further discussion** questions that promote critical thinking by asking the reader to compare and contrast aspects of the viewpoints or draw conclusions about perspectives and arguments.

- A worldwide list of **organizations to contact** for readers seeking additional information.

- A **periodical bibliography** for each chapter and a **bibliography of books** on the volume topic to aid in further research.

- A comprehensive **subject index** to offer access to people, places, events, and subjects cited in the text, with the countries covered in the viewpoints highlighted.

Global Viewpoints is designed for a broad spectrum of readers who want to learn more about current events, history, political science, government, international relations, economics, environmental science, world cultures, and sociology— students doing research for class assignments or debates, teachers and faculty seeking to supplement course materials, and others wanting to understand current issues better. By presenting how people in various countries perceive the root causes, current consequences, and proposed solutions to worldwide challenges, *Global Viewpoints* volumes offer readers opportunities to enhance their global awareness and their knowledge of cultures worldwide.

Introduction

> *"[N]ature's forces and climatic conditions cannot solely be responsible for famine causation as was the dominant mode of thinking five decades ago. Famine implies poverty, hence it cannot be understood outside of the context of poverty and poverty is as much a political issue as it is an economic concern."*
>
> —Alexander Attilio Vadala,
> *"Understanding Famine in Ethiopia:
> Poverty, Politics and Human Rights,"*
> Political Perspectives, *vol. 2, no. 1, 2008*

Since the beginning of recorded time, human beings have suffered from periodic food shortages caused by a wide variety of factors. When such food shortages extend over a sufficient period of time to cause malnutrition, starvation, and death, they are known as famines. The Christian Bible mentions famines throughout both the Old and New Testaments, and other historic records also demonstrate that famine frequently visited ancient civilizations. Famines are not limited to ancient times, however. Populations across the world, right up to the present day, continue to suffer from periods of food insecurity, shortages, and full-blown famine.

The causes of famine are many: drought, floods, crop disease, epidemics, warfare, political intrigue, soil exhaustion, overpopulation, faulty economic policies. In truth, it is nearly impossible to find just one cause of a serious famine. Nearly always, famines are caused by complicated, complex, and intertwined factors.

The Great Famine in Ireland (also known as the Great Hunger or the Irish Potato Famine) from 1845–1851 is a case in point. Ireland was under British rule at the time and largely owned by Anglo-Irish landholders. Most Irish were very poor and lived on a subsistence diet dependent on the potato. In September of 1845, the potato crop failed due to an airborne fungus that caused the potatoes to rot. Thus, the immediate cause of the Great Famine was crop failure.

The potato blight, however, was not what killed one million Irish and sent another million Irish to England and North America over the next six years. The British government and the Anglo-Irish landlords believed in a free market, arguing that the markets would eventually balance themselves. They continued to export grain from Ireland despite widespread starvation. In addition, although initially the British attempted to alleviate the food shortages by supplying cornmeal to the Irish, when the corn ran out, they shut down food relief rather than restocking. Instead, the British set up work projects wherein an Irish man could work for a day's wages building stone walls and roads. The work projects, however, were a case of the remedy being worse than the cure. The amount of money a man could earn building a wall was so little that he could not buy enough food to make up for the calories he expended by building the wall. Thus, the work projects actually accelerated the death rates from starvation; many men died on the so-called "famine roads."

Therefore, the combination of a natural disaster in the form of the potato blight, the economic oppression created by the landlord-tenant system, the "laissez faire" economic philosophy of the British government, the poverty of the Irish peasants, and racial animosity between the Catholic Irish peasants and the Protestant Anglo-Irish landowners led to disaster. The population of Ireland continued to decline due to death, lost pregnancies, disease, and infertility for over one hundred years, all as the direct result of famine. Further, as Cormac Ó Gráda and Kevin H. O'Rouke argue in *Ireland's Great Famine: Interdisciplinary Perspectives* (2008), "The Great

Famine's effects on Ireland's population were clearly permanent, rather than transitory, and emigration holds the key to understanding this." Throughout the late nineteenth and twentieth centuries, far more Irish people lived outside the borders of Ireland than within its boundaries, a trend begun during the awful famine years.

An example of a famine caused by ideology and politics occurred in China. According to Vaclav Smith writing in the *British Medical Journal*, "Between the spring of 1959 and the end of 1961 some 30 million Chinese starved to death and about the same number of births were lost or postponed." The famine was caused by Chinese leader Mao Zedong's decision that the country must engage in a "Great Leap Forward" to revitalize its economy. The goal was to increase both industrial and agricultural output. According to the United States Department of State in 2008, during the Great Leap Forward, "normal market mechanisms were disrupted, agricultural production fell behind, and China's people exhausted themselves producing what turned out to be shoddy, un-salable goods." This, combined with bad weather, resulted in what the State Department calls "one of the deadliest famines in human history."

A third example of the complicated causes of famine is that of Ethiopia. Drought and crop failures as well as a feudal form of government led to severe famine in 1984, the year that rock star Bob Geldof held his famous Band Aid and Live Aid concerts, raising nearly $150 million in relief for the nation. More than twenty years later, Ethiopia continues to be dependent on food aid from the outside world. Weather conditions have also become increasingly unstable, with a combination of drought, followed by hail, followed by heavy rains. According to the June 14, 2008, issue of *Economist*, "Meteorologists say that the problem is not just the amount of rain but the climate's increasing volatility." This, in turn, leads to repeated crop failures. In addition, groups of pastoralists who herd cattle for a living find themselves in growing competition for shrinking resources. With the rising cost of fuel and the world food shortages of 2008, many experts predict that Ethiopia will once again be the site of famine in the coming years.

Indeed, throughout Africa and the world, the dangerous combination of climate change, political maneuvering, food shortages, market instability, and the HIV/AIDS epidemic is working to create a deadly scenario, one that surely includes widespread death from starvation and famine. The viewpoints included in this book offer a global perspective on the troubling specter of famine, examining what scholar Stephen Devereux called in 2006 "the new famines," famines that persist in a world of plenty.

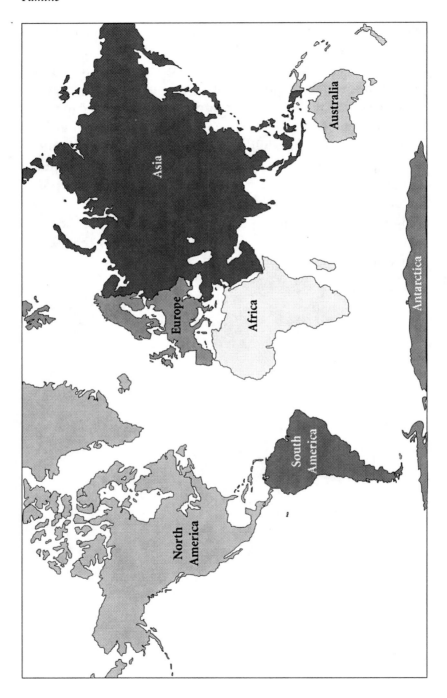

GLOBALVIEWPOINTS

CHAPTER 1

The Global Food Crisis

The Global Food Crisis: An Overview

Josette Sheeran

Josette Sheeran, the executive director of the United Nations World Food Programme, provides an overview of the world food crisis of 2007–2008. Sheeran notes with concern five key factors that are contributing to soaring food prices: the economic boom in some countries; the price of oil; the use of food crops for fuel; the increasingly severe weather; and the volatility of the agricultural futures market. Although the global food crisis is serious, it can be addressed through cooperative efforts, and can even provide opportunities for farmers from developing nations.

As you read, consider the following questions:

1. How many people does the World Food Programme help feed each year?
2. What is the World Food Programme's 80-80-80 solution for addressing the global food crisis?
3. What does the United Nations Millennium Development Goals hope to accomplish by 2015?

Food and food prices are daily headline news. News reports and images from Haiti of deadly riots triggering the collapse of the government are stark reminders that food insecurity threatens not only the hungry but peace and stability itself.

Josette Sheeran, "The New Face of Hunger: Keynote Address," Center for Strategic and International Studies, Washington, DC, April 18, 2008. www.csis.org. © 2008 Center for Strategic & International Studies. All rights reserved. Reproduced by permission.

Yesterday [April 17, 2008] South Africa joined 33 other nations that have seen thousands of hungry people pour onto the streets demanding relief. As I talk with farmers and consumers in the developing world, they express confusion and frustration as to what is robbing them of milk for their children, their weekly portion of meat, or, for those who make less than 50 cents a day, reducing them to a single bowl of grain or one piece of bread a day. With little awareness of the macroeconomic forces at play, many blame their own leaders and local suppliers, millers, traders and anyone else—threatening confidence in fragile democracies and markets. The world's misery index is rising as soaring food and fuel prices roll through the lives of the most vulnerable; a silent tsunami that respects no borders. Most do not know what has hit them.

The world [has] been consuming more than it produced, with food stocks being drawn down to their lowest levels in [at] least three decades.

A New Face of Hunger

With the price of rice rising by 75 percent in just the past two months [since February 2008], and wheat rising by 120 percent over the year, the world's most vulnerable are getting hit hard. The issue here is resiliency, and for those living on less than 50 cents a day there is no place to retreat. There is a new face of hunger, with people who were not in the urgent category just months ago, joining the ranks of desperation.

[Nobel Prize-winning economist] Amartya Sen's groundbreaking [1981] work studying famines found they are, at their root, caused by the disparity of food prices, which rise rapidly during a disaster, while family income declines and traditional coping methods become exhausted. The World Bank estimates that these rapidly accelerating prices will drive

100 million people into more extreme poverty and places 33 nations at risk of instability due to soaring prices.

Joachim von Braun, the Director General of the International Food Policy Research Institute, warns that developing nations, especially net food importers, are being hit hardest. He says: "The world food system is in trouble and the hot spots of food risks will be where high food prices combine with shocks from weather or political crises. These are recipes for disaster."

United States Agriculture Secretary Ed Schafer said this week that the world has never been "less secure about the near term future of wheat as crop failure and disease combine to threaten food supply; US wheat stocks are at a 60 year low." The Secretary General of the United Nations has declared a global food emergency, and the head of the World Bank has called for a "new deal" on global food policy. The President of El Salvador has called this a perfect storm, and the Prime Minister of India said this will threaten India's economic growth and poverty reduction. . . .

The World Food Programme

The World Food Programme [WFP] is the world's largest humanitarian organization and charged with the responsibility to meet the urgent call of hunger when all other systems collapse. Today we reach up to 90 million people a year threatened with starvation and acute malnutrition. We are also among the most efficient in the world, using only seven percent of our budget on overhead. WFP is 100 percent voluntarily funded; receiving no assessed funds from any source. When WFP was founded, it literally was a surplus food program with nations of the world sharing their bounty with the world's hungry. This saved many millions of lives, but also could be a rather blunt instrument, leading at times to a mismatch between populations and food products and could lead to disruptions in local agricultural markets. Today, less than two percent of our food is surplus donation.

WFP has evolved and in June I will present to our Board a new strategic plan marking a historic transition from a food-aid agency to a food-assistance agency. What I mean by that is looking at how we can use food and food assistance to break the cycle of hunger at its roots to help be part of the long term solution. . . .

Solving Hunger at the Local Level

For example, today half of WFP's budget is cash, and we use 80 percent of that cash to purchase food from small farmers in 69 developing nations, creating win-win solutions to hunger and malnutrition. . . . I will just give a quick example in Senegal [in western Africa] where there is a huge problem with goiter because virtually none of the salt for local consumption is iodized. They have big salt producing companies that do iodize but it all gets exported. WFP decided that we would purchase our salt for our programs in Senegal from 7,000 village salt producers and, working with the Micronutrient Initiative we helped them get credit for the equipment and training in the technology to iodize the salt.

> Rice consumption has outpaced production for the past few decades, cutting global rice reserves by half since 2000.

Today those 7,000 salt producers—most of them women—have a steady income and they provide 100 percent of the salt needs for our Senegal program. In fact, they now produce iodized salt for the local markets, which is helping address what President Wade called one of the biggest health challenges in Senegal. This is a win-win situation. The salt-ladies of Senegal are so good that we were able to now buy some of our salt for our regional programs from them.

This is the kind of win-win solution that we feel can use food assistance to break hunger at its root. These solutions require a team effort; all of us pulling together. Not only the Rome-based UN agencies, but throughout the global system—governments, NGOs [non-governmental organizations], villagers—working together. There are hundreds of such examples. Today, in our school feeding program in Ghana [in western Africa], 100 percent of the food is purchased locally. When floods devastated Mozambique this year, we procured 70 percent of the food for victims locally.

I call this part of my 80-80-80 solution: 80 percent of WFP's cash for food is spent in the developing world; 80 percent of our land transportation is procured in the developing world from local contractors; and 80 percent of my more than 10,000 staff is locally hired. This infuses more than $612 million into local farmer economies and more than $2 billion a year overall into developing world economies. This helps build capacity at the local level for food security infrastructure, food production and food policy expertise. . . .

Worrisome Trends in Global Food Markets

Soon after joining WFP a year ago, I looked at our portfolio of work and became very concerned about trends in global food markets. The cost of food had been steadily increasing, reversing over four decades of declining prices. I saw that the world was consuming more than it produced, with food stocks being drawn down to their lowest levels in [at] least three decades, reducing the stock-to-use ratio from around 120 days of supply to one third that number.

I looked at increasingly severe weather events that were significantly impacting harvests from Australia to West Africa to Bangladesh, with climate change portending even worse. I said at the time that we were facing a potential "perfect storm" for the world's most vulnerable, and thought that we had a few years early warning. However, in June [2007], prices started accelerating even more, with WFP's average global purchase price for grain rising 55 percent from June to this February [2008]. This pattern of aggressive increases has continued. On March 3 [2008], WFP was paying $460 for a metric ton of rice in Asia, last week [April 2008] the cost was $780 a metric ton. I believe that we are now in the eye of the storm. If you look at some of the factors driving this storm, most experts predict they will be with us for some time.

A confluence of factors is responsible for aggressively soaring commodity prices. At its core, this is a supply and demand challenge. For example, rice consumption has outpaced production for the past few decades, cutting global rice reserves by half since 2000. Food supply is relatively inflexible and vulnerable to unpredictable factors such as weather. All global stocks have drawn down to the lowest levels in decades. I will briefly touch on five factors which present the world with both challenges and opportunities.

The total number of disasters worldwide on average is now 400–500 a year, up from an average of 125 in the 1980s.

Challenges and Opportunities

First, is the economic boom in some parts of the developing world. This means people in emerging economies, including in China, India, Brazil and more than ten growth leaders in Africa, are changing their diet, as others have done throughout history as they have become more prosperous. China has almost doubled its consumption of meat, fish and dairy products since 1990. This takes a lot of grain off global markets, since, for example, it takes seven pounds of grain to produce one pound of meat. This increased demand in China reached a tipping point over the past few years, with China disappearing as one of the largest maize exporters in the world, into an importer of maize virtually overnight.

The second factor is the price of oil, which as the head of WFP, I look to the price of oil every day to determine how much hunger there will be in the world. It has reached record highs this week [April 18, 2008] at $115 a barrel. This drives up costs across the entire value chain of food production— from fertilizer, to diesel for tilling, planting and harvesting, to storage and shipping. High oil prices also make food a financially attractive input for industrial use.

The third factor is the global linking of food and fuel markets. As farmers all over the world know, advanced production techniques for biofuels and biodeisel, combined with the high price of oil make feedstock an increasingly attractive input for industrialized use. This is a global phenomenon, affecting markets for wheat, maize, sugar, oil seeds, cassava, palm oil and beyond.

Fourth is increasingly severe weather. According to USAID's [United States Agency for International Development's] Office of Foreign Disaster Assistance, the total number of disasters worldwide on average is now 400–500 a year, up from an average of 125 in the 1980s. This has affected WFP. In the 1980s, 80 percent of WFP's work was developmental and 20 percent emergency. We have now reversed that rate—80 percent of our work is emergency, often responding to natural disasters.

Almost half the world's hungry are marginalized farmers with little or no access to fertilizer, seeds, tractors, credit, markets, or extension services.

The dramatic increase in futures markets and hedging on agricultural products is increasing the price volatility and reactive policies are creating even tighter supplies by shutting down exports. Today, one third of the globe's wheat suppliers, have banned exports. . . .

Why Rice Prices Are Skyrocketing

Rice prices have been rising steadily on world markets since 2003. The underlying factors behind this trend in recent years are similar to those pushing up other food prices. Four basic drivers seem to stimulate rapid growth in demand for food commodities: first, rising living standards in China, India and other rapidly growing developing countries, which lead to increased demand for livestock products and the feedstuffs to produce them; second, stimulus from mandates for corn-based ethanol in the US and the ripple effects beyond the corn economy that are stimulated by inter-commodity linkages; third, the rapid depreciation of the US dollar against the euro and a number of other important currencies, which drives up the price of commodities priced in US dollars; and finally, increased speculation from new financial players searching for better returns than in stocks or real estate. Underneath all of these demand drivers is the high price of petroleum and other fossil fuels.

C. Peter Trimmer, "Japan Ducks Rice-Crisis Solution,"
Asia Times, July 18, 2008. www.atimes.com.

I am a medium- to long-term optimist. At its root, increased demand should be an opportunity. This perfect storm has dramatically raised awareness that food cannot and must not be taken for granted. Food, to the shock of many, does not spontaneously appear on grocery food shelves. The fact that the food supply chain, from imports, to planting, to harvesting, to processing, to storage and delivery, and all the supporting market structures, from access to credit, risk mitigation, commodity exchanges, crop surveys, and water access are all vital to world stability and prosperity, is something that the world is waking up to.

It has also raised awareness that we have to prepare for the challenges of climate change, which the IPCC [Intergovernmental Panel on Climate Change] predicts that some food insecure areas of the world, particularly in rain-dependent nations of Africa, could produce half the yield in the next 12 years that they are producing today.

But also, this is an opportunity, not only for the American farmer, but hopefully for poor farmers in Latin America, Asia, Africa and elsewhere. Seventy percent of African farmers are women, and they often bear more of the risk and receive less of the gain for their efforts than any farmer in the world. In fact, almost half the world's hungry are marginalized farmers with little or no access to fertilizer, seeds, tractors, credit, markets, or extension services. Perhaps, as I mentioned to African finance ministers last week at the African Union, the time has finally come for the African farmer.

Let us take today's global food crisis as an early warning and an incentive to revolutionizing agricultural policies and investment, and access to the science and technologies that can defeat hunger once and for all.

Now, on to the challenges; first, in a time of increased need, WFP is able to reach fewer people than even just months ago. Due solely to soaring prices, today WFP has 40 percent less food in the pipeline than in June [2007] for the same level of contribution. For our programs, this is a direct impact. I was just in Kenya, in the Kibera slums, at a school where many of the children rely on WFP for their only cup of food each day.

One Cup of Food Per Day

Some of you have seen my red cup before—this is Lillian's cup from one of our school feeding programs in Rwanda. If you travel throughout the developing world you will see these cups in the schools where WFP is partnering with governments in reaching 20 million children. When I was in Kibera, for many of the children it was the only cup of food they get a day. That is vulnerability. Also, we have found that often the children take half of the food home for siblings who have no food.

Today, this cup can get filled 40 percent less due simply to soaring prices. Without increased donations, all of WFP's work is threatened with a 40 percent reduction in the coming weeks. That is why we have put out an emergency appeal to the world—an extraordinary appeal. WFP must raise its core budget of $2.9 billion, and our emergency "gap" appeal which when I announced in February [2008] was $500 million. Since that announcement, the gap has increased to $755 million. Neither of these numbers includes new needs.

If a child does not eat adequate nutrition in the first two years of life, he or she is mentally and physically disadvantaged for life.

Second, right now we have an emerging new face of hunger as discussed. Many are being driven into greater poverty and malnutrition. This is hitting poor households hard. Those living on $2 a day, we are seeing give up education and health care expenditures in order to afford basic food. At $1 a day, people are giving up protein and any kind of additions to their diet like vegetables. At 50 cents a day—which includes 160 million people—there is no place to retreat. So if they are already just eating three bowls of grain a day, you cut that down to two or one.

The most vulnerable are import-dependent nations, which includes most of Africa, and—by the way—most of the world. The vast majority of nations are food importers. If you take an import-dependent nation and add one more shock like the cyclone in Bangladesh or the floods in West Africa we find people driven to desperation.

Among the emerging new face of hunger, we have already clocked in new emergency requests, such as the emergency appeal we issued with the Government of Afghanistan in January for 2.5 million newly hungry people priced out of food markets, at a cost of $77 million. Since January, there are almost half a billion dollars in new needs identified.

Third, we are concerned about access to food supplies. For example, we tried to buy wheat this fall to make biscuits for the victims of the floods in DPRK [Democratic People's Republic of Korea] and for 10 days, and for the first time in memory, we could not buy it anywhere in the markets in Asia. In the past few weeks we have had five of our commodity contracts broken. Between the time we made the contract and picking up the food two weeks later, prices had risen so quickly that the grain went to a higher bidder, with the supplier willingly paying WFP the five percent performance bonds to get out of our contract.

Farmers Cannot Afford to Plant Crops

The fourth is connected to that. This is a new observation based on my recent travels to Africa. One would expect that the natural reaction from farmers to high prices would be to plant more. In the developing world, there are indications that the reverse is happening. I knew that most poor farmers were not benefiting from the high prices because half the hungry in Africa are farmers who cannot even produce enough for their own family. Most are so disconnected from markets that they really cannot benefit. What I did not realize and what I saw in Africa is that many are planting less, not more than before, because they cannot afford the inputs.

In Kenya, fertilizer has gone from 1,700 shillings in December to 4,000 shillings just 12 weeks later. Last week I went to the Rift Valley—the breadbasket of Kenya—and they were planting one-third of what they were planting a year ago. According to the *International Herald Tribune* this is happening in Laos, and IFAD [International Fund for Agricultural Development] says they see this happening throughout the developing world. These farmers are retreating to subsistence mode, withdrawing from markets until things stabilize. This could indicate serious shortages in upcoming harvests, further compounding the global challenge.

The BBC interviewed a reporter from Haiti this week who said, in effect, that "There's no room for error here. Things could go bad really quickly. Desperation's growing quickly." I talked to a member of Congress who said he ran for Congress as a medical doctor, because he had come to understand that there are only seven meals between civilization and anarchy. Meaning at the seventh meal lost, things fall apart.

My fifth concern I will outline here is that many of the policy reactions globally and locally may actually be helping feed the crisis, not people. It is understandable that nations will use whatever levers they have to alleviate pressure. Yet some of these may deepen the challenge. Today, many of the world's farmers are under price controls, further discouraging increased planting. Inputs rise, but food prices are under a ceiling. A range of major food exporters have put blocks on food exports almost overnight, from China, to Vietnam, to Argentina, to Kazakhstan. This global rash of "beggar thy neighbor" responses will not provide a solution.

What Should Be Done?

We must take this crisis as a global call to action. The first [United Nations] Millennium Development Goal [MDG] calls for cutting the proportion of hungry by half by 2015. I call this MDG the "gateway" MDG because there is no way to achieve any other hopes and dreams for humanity unless people have access to adequate nutrition. It is the most basic human right; without food one is denied life itself. Today, there is a global malnutrition crisis where one in every three children in the developing world is stunted. According to the landmark series in *The Lancet* this January, if a child does not get adequate nutrition in the first two years of life, he or she is mentally and physically disadvantaged for life. Hunger and malnutrition can be defeated and the world knows how to do it. Many countries have made vast progress, breaking hunger at its root, including the country of my ancestors—Ireland. In addition, we must look to the plight of the smallholder farmer and develop medium- and long-term supply-side solutions. My hope is that the time has come for the poor smallholder farmer, the African farmer, to see the kind of investment that can break the cycle of poverty. So I join with FAO [the United Nations Food and Agriculture Organization], the World Bank, IFAD and others in calling for a 'twin-track' response to meet the emergency needs but also to step up the supply-side solutions.

First, we must help governments alleviate immediate suffering and prevent a crippling outbreak of severe malnutrition that could set global development back by decades. When there is no food to be had, we must keep the humanitarian pipeline full. . . . We have tools now where we can reach children under the age of two, and alleviate an acute malnutrition crisis virtually overnight. We also have long-term expertise in helping countries design price stabilization programs and safety net programs, such as we are doing in Egypt to help the government with its crisis there. We also have experience using cash and voucher interventions. As we are seeing in this "new face of hunger," sometimes people cannot afford food off the shelves, they need cash or voucher help for a targeted, short period of time, and we have done some of that in Indonesia after the economic crisis there.

We are working with the Howard Buffett Foundation and the Gates Foundation and others to look at our local purchase and how we can use our contracts to help drive the long term solutions. For example, right now, we are exploring the possibilities of giving farmers forward contracts to be able to get credit, to be able to get better seed, and to be able to get more fertilizer to help break the cycle of low yields and poverty so we will not have to be in there year after year. We are looking at launching a major program to look at the way we do business and to do it in a way that can really help. This has helped in places like the DRC [Democratic Republic of the Congo] which, as I mentioned, is at war, but we are buying from those farmers completely cut-off from markets due to the conflicts. We can go in there with our logistical strength, and also help them get access to markets in a very powerful way.

An Australian Perspective on the Global Food Crisis

David Nason

David Nason, a correspondent for The Australian *newspaper, contends that food inflation is leading the way to serious famine across the globe. He blames the inflation on dietary changes in China, drought, speculation in international markets, and export restrictions. He also calls the impact of food inflation on the world's poor disastrous. Finally, he asserts that ethanol production is using food crops that should be feeding people rather than fueling cars.*

As you read, consider the following questions:

1. What countries had food riots in the six weeks before this viewpoint was written?
2. How are people who earn $1 per day coping with food inflation?
3. What did British Prime Minister Gordon Brown say about mandated biofuel targets in his country?

It's 40 years since Stanford University entomologist Paul Ehrlich predicted that hundreds of millions of people would die of starvation in the 1970s and '80s because the world could no longer produce enough food for its rapidly growing population.

David Nason, "First Signs of the Coming Famine," *The Australian*, June 7, 2008. www.theaustralian.news.com.au. Copyright © 2008 News Limited. Reproduced by permission.

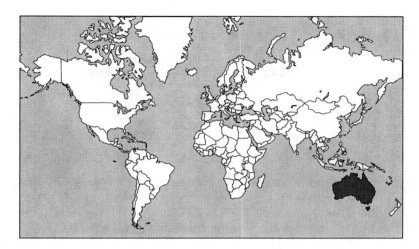

Ehrlich outlined his theories in *The Population Bomb*, a bestseller that offered policy prescriptions ranging from compulsory birth control, cutting government payments for dependent children, applying a luxury tax to cribs and nappies, and ceasing food aid to the third world.

Not surprisingly, Ehrlich was branded a crackpot and his basic premise that a terrible age of famine was at hand never eventuated. In fact, there was less famine in the last quarter of the 20th century than at any time in history, the result of world food production growing at 15 per cent annually and outstripping the growth in population.

The famines that did occur arose from natural catastrophes or the interruption of food supply and cultivation in war zones.

Famine Is Expanding

But today, with the cost of staples such as rice, corn, wheat and soybeans skyrocketing, with food riots breaking out across the globe and with the UN's [United Nations'] World Food Programme warning of a "silent tsunami" of hunger threatening the lives of 20 million of the world's poorest children, gal-

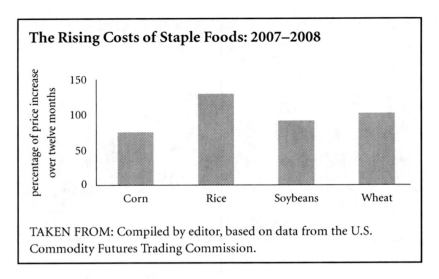

The Rising Costs of Staple Foods: 2007–2008

percentage of price increase over twelve months

TAKEN FROM: Compiled by editor, based on data from the U.S. Commodity Futures Trading Commission.

loping food inflation is raising Ehrlich-like fears of a world where famine is no longer confined to war zones and sub-Saharan Africa.

Over the past six weeks [April 16, 2008] the UN has reported food riots in Egypt, Yemen, Ethiopia, Cameroon, Bangladesh, Malaysia, Indonesia, Cote d'Ivoire, Mauritania, Mozambique and Senegal. In the worst case in Haiti, five people died and prime minister Jacques-Edouard Alexis was forced from office.

Rice shortages have led to Cambodia and Egypt banning rice exports, China imposing heavy export taxes and many other countries including Malaysia, Singapore, Sri Lanka and the Philippines begin stockpiling.

The World Bank estimates that prices for all foods have risen 83 percent in the past three years.

Manila has also asked fast-food multinationals such as McDonald's to serve half-portions of rice, while Pakistan and Russia have raised wheat export taxes by 35 per cent and 40 per cent respectively.

Other countries with new restrictions on grain exports include Brazil, Argentina and Vietnam. India has blocked export of all rice except premium basmati, while Guinea has banned the export of all foodstuffs.

Soaring Food Prices

According to the US [United States] Commodity Futures Trading Commission, the price of rice over the past 12 months has soared a staggering 122 per cent. For wheat, the increase has been 95 per cent, for soybeans 83 per cent and corn 66 per cent. The World Bank estimates that prices for all foods have risen 83 per cent in the past three years.

This week, UN food envoy Jean Ziegler blamed these price explosions on Wall Street, saying a herd of market traders, speculators and financial bandits had "turned wild and constructed a world of inequality and horror". But greed and opportunism on financial markets is only part of the story.

Food inflation is also about recent droughts in Australia and Russia; changing eating patterns in China and India, where the burgeoning middle classes want to eat more grain-fed meat and dairy products; the chronically weak US dollar; flawed alternative energy policies in the US and EU [European Union]; and the blowout in the cost of fuel and fertiliser.

Eating Mud in Haiti

Above all else, food inflation is about the hunger of the poor, and if there's one anecdote that drives home the desperate suffering, it's the story of mothers in Haitian slums who have been feeding their children mud pies mixed with oil and sugar to try to make their hunger pangs go away.

"There's something really massively wrong when people are forced to eat mud," says Seton Hall University law professor and freedom from hunger activist Frank Pasquale. "The world simply cannot sit and watch this happen. People like (Indian economist) Amartya Sen might say there has never been a famine in a democracy but what we're seeing here could be a world first. I mean, we've had food riots in relatively well-ordered societies like Egypt and Malaysia. That tells us there could be a huge challenge just ahead."

Treasurer Wayne Swan was struck by the same realisation at the International Monetary Fund's recent meeting in Washington. Expecting conversations away from the formal agenda to revolve around the troubles in the US housing and credit markets, Swan was surprised to find food inflation the dominant topic.

When he sat next to Indian Finance Minister Shri Chidambaram at lunch on the final day, the subject was rice shortages, not Australian uranium.

The Practical Implications of Food Inflation

In a cover story this month, *The Economist* explained the practical impact of food inflation in poor countries.

"The middle classes are giving up health care and cutting out meat so they can eat three meals a day," the magazine said.

"The middling poor, those on $US2 a day, are pulling children from school and cutting back on vegetables so they can still afford rice. Those on $US1 a day are cutting back on meat, vegetables and one or two meals so they can afford one bowl. The desperate—those on 50c[ents] a day—face disaster."

It's estimated that filling the fuel tank of a standard four-wheel-drive with ethanol uses the same amount of corn that would feed a child for a year.

Given that one billion of the world's six billion people live on $US1 a day and another 1.5 billion exist on $US1 to $US2 a day, any extended period of high food prices would be devastating.

According to World Bank president Robert Zoellick and UN secretary-general Ban Ki-moon, the improvements made in the lives of the world's poorest one billion people over the past decade would be wiped out. And Zoellick has warned that the political stability of 33 nations is in peril if the situation doesn't soon improve.

But for many the urgency needed is lacking. In the US, provider of 50 per cent of the world's food aid dollars, the Bush administration's response has been limited to providing an extra $US200 million ($213million) in urgent aid and asking Congress to amend the Farm Bill so that one-quarter of US food aid can be spent on local and regional procurement.

While this would allow faster, more flexible deployment of vital aid dollars, save millions of dollars in unnecessary transport costs and feed more hungry people, it threatens powerful farm interests in Washington, who want food-aid dollars spent in the US. The measure is far from a sure thing.

Ethanol Production Causes Food Price Inflation

But the biggest failure of US policy concerns the huge subsidies being paid to farmers to grow corn for the ethanol industry. This year one-third of the US corn crop will be diverted into making ethanol. And as more and more land is set aside for ethanol production, prices for other crops such as soybeans and cotton are rising.

It's estimated that filling the fuel tank of a standard four-wheel-drive with ethanol uses the same amount of corn that would feed a child for a year.

"Grain-based ethanol production here or anywhere in the world is just not sustainable," says Democrat Congressman Ron Kind of Wisconsin. "We have to make that leap to cellulose and develop that enzyme to make it economically feasible. And we've got to do it soon."

Kind also believes the high prices for agricultural commodities make it the perfect time to get rid of many of the subsidies enjoyed by US farmers, and pass a Farm Bill that is less market and trade distorting.

"There's no reason we can't do that, other than powerful, entrenched special interests in Washington who are fighting us all the way," he says. "That's the problem. You've got a big biofuels kick in this country, with a lot of build-up of ethanol plants and more income for farmers."

Pasquale agrees the quest for biofuels can't be allowed to ride roughshod over the lives of the world's poorest people, but he remains troubled by the complex politics involved. "You have good people who are very concerned about global warming but who find the only way to get political support is through a corrupt bargain with people in farm states in the US," he says.

This week British Prime Minister Gordon Brown, previously an advocate of ethanol, switched horses, saying that mandated biofuel targets—in Britain's case 5 per cent of transport fuel by 2010—needed to be reviewed everywhere in the light of the food inflation crisis and the need to use land for food rather than energy production.

Even so, Kind wants the US to continue protecting 14m ha [14 million hectares, roughly over 30 million acres] of idle farmland that farmers are being paid $US1.8 billion a year not to cultivate. "This is highly sensitive, erosion-prone land that is not conducive to agricultural production," he says.

The Developed World May Experience Food Shortages

Richard North

Parliamentary researcher and author Richard North argues that rapidly rising food prices in the United Kingdom are a part of the global food crisis. He asserts that demand for food has outstripped supply, and that millions of people in the developing world are headed for starvation. Further, he believes, Western politically driven notions of how to solve the crisis are likely to cause more harm than good. Instead, he asserts, the only solution is to provide assistance to third world farmers in the form of modern agriculture. Otherwise, the food shortages will reach developed nations as well.

As you read, consider the following questions:

1. What has undermined the profitability of farming in Britain?
2. According to North, what was the result of the ban on the pesticide DDT in Africa?
3. How should Western aid be distributed, according to North?

In our television age, the mention of a food crisis brings to mind the bloated bellies of starving children.

We think of droughts, crop failure, conflicts and the tub-thumping of Bono and Bob Geldof.

Richard North, "How the Era of Cheap Food Has Gone and Why We Face a Hungry Future," *MailOnline*, April 26, 2008. www.mailonsunday.co.uk. © 2008 Associated Newspapers Ltd. Reproduced by permission.

But now we have a very different sort of food crisis, one that last week [April 2008] for the first time brought food rationing to America when the supermarket giant Wal-Mart—owner of Asda—restricted customers to four bags of rice per visit.

The United Kingdom Faces High Food Prices

We are not immune in this country. The cost of a granary [bread] loaf at Waitrose [a British supermarket] is inextricably linked to massive hikes in global food prices.

Wheat has doubled to £200 per ton. The wholesale price of rice has soared 70 per cent.

> *By the simple laws of supply and demand, prices have gone through the roof.*

And it is prices like these, rather than shortages, that have triggered food riots in Egypt, Mexico, Haiti—where the government was brought down—the Philippines, Bangladesh and China.

The Food Crisis and Global Politics

Make no mistake, the current food crisis has the capacity to transform global politics. There is nothing more fundamental than food.

In Britain, rising grain prices have already undermined the profitability of poultry and livestock farms.

Good-quality food will become the preserve of the well-off, while those on lower incomes will have to make do with what they can afford.

The chasm between rich and poor will widen further, with all the implications for domestic strife that has.

In the developing world, where hundreds of millions are already struggling to get by, the food crisis threatens to undo all the advances of the past two decades.

Untold millions could be forced if not into starvation, then into hunger, malnutrition and misery.

Conflict and global instability will increase. If you thought the world was unstable now, we could soon be looking back on this as a golden age of tranquillity.

Third World aid is almost always counter-productive in the long run—it serves only to fuel corruption, prop up despotic regimes and undermine fragile economies.

So serious is the situation that [British] Prime Minister Gordon Brown last week called an emergency summit of leading experts, including the head of the UN's [United Nations'] World Food Programme.

He declared that the food crisis threatened 'to roll back progress made in recent years to lift millions of people out of poverty'. Millions more were promised in Third World aid.

But Western intervention on current lines is likely to be futile when the causes of the crisis are complex, global—and likely to be permanent.

Indeed, using the simplistic logic of the Western aid industry, there should be no problem at all.

Despite poor harvests in drought-stricken Australia, last year's [2007] global grain crop broke all records.

At 2.3 billion tons, it beat the previous year's total by almost 5 per cent.

Causes of the Food Crisis

So why the crisis? Some accuse hedge funds—burnt by the "credit crunch" and property crash—of moving billions into food and driving prices beyond the reach of the poor.

But more important than any speculative bubble is the simple fact that consumption has outstripped even this record harvest.

World Population Estimates from 1900 to 2050

Year	Population (in millions)
1900	1,650
1910	1,750
1920	1,860
1930	2,070
1940	2,300
1950	2,519
1960	3,023
1970	3,696
1980	4,440
1990	5,279
2000	6,085
2010 (projected)	6,842
2020 (projected)	7,577
2040 (projected)	8,701
2050 (projected)	9,075

TAKEN FROM: "Historical World Population Estimates," Population Reference Bureau, 2008. www.prb.org.

By the simple laws of supply and demand, prices have gone through the roof.

The demand has been fuelled by an evermore populous and prosperous developing world.

And this is bringing a seismic change analogous to the oil shocks of the seventies or the 19th century population shift from the countryside to towns.

Food prices will always fluctuate with global markets, but the era of food so cheap that we in the West never even had to think about it has gone for good.

In simple terms, the world population doubled between 1961 and 1986 and is still growing at the rate of 75 million people a year.

Food production has largely kept up, but the gains in production are slowing.

A further factor is the rising affluence of the emergent middle classes in China and India and the associated increase in the demand for meat—though this is, as yet, a relatively minor effect.

The Response of the Western World

So what have we in the West done about it?

We have made matters worse by instigating a completely artificial rush to convert food into biofuel to drive our cars—a policy initially driven by a US desire to reduce its energy dependence on volatile Middle East states. Now the EU [European Union] has joined in, using a so-called green agenda to promote biofuels to try to mitigate carbon emissions and control global warming.

Already, 100 million tons of food a year is being diverted to make biofuel.

And in the week when Mr Brown convened his crisis meeting, a new EU target came into force—that 2.5 per cent of petrol and diesel should be replaced by biofuel.

This is set to rise to 10 per cent by 2020, adding massively to the pressure on food production.

Unless we act now it is only a matter of time before we see empty supermarkets and real shortages of food, even in the developed world.

The European Union Ban on Pesticides Costs African Lives

Another well-meaning EU initiative wrapped in "green" clothing is the ban on cheap, effective pesticides.

More than half of the global harvest is lost to pests and plant disease, yet EU legislation has outlawed the majority of the pesticides on the market.

New laws could wipe out 95 per cent of the remaining 250 or so and make the development of new products prohibitively expensive.

This [is] not an academic problem.

The eighties ban on DDT [a potent pesticide]—which even the World Health Organisation now admits was misplaced—has cost Africa up to £50billion in lost production and resulted in the deaths of 30 million people.

But then Western politicians have always been driven more by a need to announce grand new initiatives than by logic.

Third World aid is almost always counter-productive in the long run—it serves only to fuel corruption, prop up despotic regimes and undermine fragile local economies.

Meanwhile, import tariffs and trade barriers prevent poor farmers getting full market prices—and they also penalise consumers, who have to pay over the odds for staple foodstuffs.

Rethinking the Western Response to Hunger

If we are to tackle this food crisis effectively, we in the West have to rethink how we help the 840 million people said to be in chronic hunger.

As well as liberalising trade, we need to encourage increased agricultural productivity.

Only farmers can solve the global food crisis, and to help them achieve this we need to make them more efficient.

Countries with successful agriculture sectors invariably have proper, enforceable systems of land rights, so small farmers can borrow against the value of their land to modernise production and increase yields.

The disastrous example of [President Robert] Mugabe's Zimbabwe makes it clear what is likely to happen when land rights are destroyed.

Poverty-stricken nations need the rule of law, not the pity of rich neighbours in the West. We need to be tough.

Western aid should be conditional on the introduction of effective land rights.

And it should bypass governments to be distributed through agricultural banks providing small loans direct to small farmers.

It has already happened here—Western agriculture has been transformed since the Second World War thanks to mechanisation, fertilisers, pesticides and high-yield seed.

Now Third World farmers need to be given access to modern growing techniques. World food markets can be stabilised. But the situation is urgent.

Unless we act now it is only a matter of time before we see empty supermarkets and real shortages of food, even in the developed world.

A Jamaican Perspective on the Global Food Crisis

Keeble McFarlane

In a response to the Food and Agriculture Organization's June 2008 meeting in Rome, Italy, to discuss the world food crisis, Keeble McFarlane contends that there is tremendous waste of food around the globe. In addition, he notes that there is growing pressure on the world's food supply. He argues that the problem of world hunger could be addressed simply by citizens of wealthy countries not wasting food. McFarlane is a Jamaican living in Canada who writes a regular column for The Jamaica Observer.

As you read, consider the following questions:

1. To what does McFarlane attribute the growing pressure on the world's food supply?
2. How many people does McFarlane say do not have enough food?
3. What is a "Hoover plate," according to McFarlane?

F ood was on the agenda for three days in Rome this week [June 3–5, 2008], as more than 40 heads of state and government and representatives of many other countries gathered in Rome to try to figure out how to deal with the food crisis now facing the world.

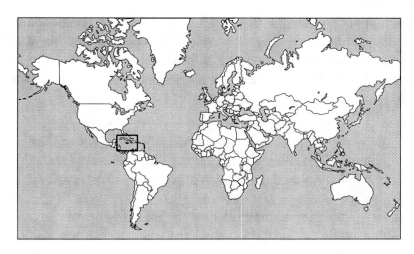

The Food and Agriculture Organisation [FAO], one of the UN's [United Nations'] specialised agencies, was host of the conference, and in his opening statement, the director-general, Jacques Diouf, appealed to world leaders for $30 billion [U.S.] a year to beef up agriculture to meet demand. Diouf pointed out that two years ago, the world spent $1.2 trillion [U.S.] on arms, while just one country could throw away $100-billion worth of food. More tellingly, he noted, obese people consume some US$20 billion in food each year, yet, "How can we explain to people of good sense and good faith that it is not possible to find $30 billion a year to enable 862 million hungry people to enjoy the most fundamental of human rights—the right to food and the right to life?"

Discontent and Disorder over Food Shortages

In recent months, countries in various parts of the world have experienced discontent and disorder over shortages in supply and dramatically increased prices for food. There are severe pressures on the world's food supply, some from population increase, but there are others. Improved economic conditions in the developing world are putting increased pressure on the food supply as people demand more choices in their diet, including more meat. The diversion of food crops, notably corn, to manufacture fuel for vehicles is another factor, and the increased interest by commodity exchanges in food as a trading item has sent up prices drastically.

Each day people throw away 660,000 eggs, 1.6 million bananas, 7 million slices of bread, 2.8 million tomatoes, 1.2 million sausages, 200,000 packages of cheese and 700,000 packages of chocolate.

Starvation is not the problem it once was, but hunger certainly is. As the FAO chief stated, almost one-sixth of the people in the world don't have enough food, and that number could grow dramatically, if something isn't done soon. But there's another aspect of the world's food supply which affects every country—rich and poor—and which happens right before our eyes, but which goes almost unnoticed.

Wasting Food

Those of us who do have enough to eat contribute significantly to the food problem by the amount we waste. I recall an incident some 20-odd years ago in Toronto when I joined a colleague for lunch at a popular buffet restaurant. We sat at a table on an elevated platform which ran around the perimeter of the room, and as the patrons left to return to work, we gazed out over a sea of tables filled with discarded salads, slices of beef, chicken legs, whole potatoes, untouched rolls and hundreds of pats of butter. My colleague remarked, "Can you imagine, this scene is repeated all across North America right now!"

Around the same time I met a young woman who was trying to break into acting and like so many others in that trade took a job waitressing to pay the bills. She lived in a modest apartment in a rooming house near to a market dis-

---

Food Waste in the United States

Official surveys indicate that every year more than 350 billion pounds (160 billion kg) of edible food are available for human consumption in the United States. Of that total, nearly 100 billion pounds (45 billion kg)—including fresh vegetables, fruits, milk, and grain products—are lost to waste by retailers, restaurants, and consumers.

Haider Rizvi,
"US: Food Waste and Hunger Exist Side by Side,"
Common Dreams News Center, September 4, 2004.
www.commondreams.org.

---

trict and every night on the way home checked the garbage cans outside the green-grocer shops to raid the stuff they had put out. She would fish out her collapsible bag and stuff it with cabbages which suffered from nothing but a few wilted leaves. Turnips, tomatoes, potatoes—you name it—went into her bag. She boasted that her food bill was extremely bearable as a result. The most she had to do was cut out the small blemishes which prompted the grocers to throw out the otherwise perfectly good produce.

The British waste more food than any other nation—throwing out as much as 40 percent of all they produce and buy.

All Are Guilty

Supermarkets, wholesalers, food manufacturers and even farmers are equally guilty of wasting food. Vendors think they can't present anything, but the most attractive items to customers, and routinely dump bananas, apples, tomatoes, heads of lettuce or whatever because they aren't perfect. Farmers in wealthy countries often plough harvested food back into the ground if they produce more than they have contracted for to wholesalers. Food suppliers discard items which have reached their expiry dates, even though the food is still edible. And householders contribute their share of the wastage.

In Britain, an organisation called Waste and Resources Action Programme, or WRAP, estimates that each day people throw away 660,000 eggs, 1.6 million bananas, 7 million slices of bread, 2.8 million tomatoes, 1.2 million sausages, 200,000 packages of cheese and 700,000 packages of chocolate. That's every day! A couple of years ago the *Guardian* newspaper conducted a survey and concluded that the British waste more food than any other nation—throwing out as much as 40 per cent of all they produce and buy. The paper reported that this adds up to as much as £16 billion [about $32 billion U.S.] a year. It said this was way ahead of the US, which is also no slouch in wasting food—there the figure is estimated at $100 billion a year.

The Hoover Plate

Some experts say the problem is that even though the cost of food is rising, and will do so dramatically in the next little while, food in many countries is still relatively cheap and easy to come by, and is, therefore, treated as a mere commodity. This was not always the case, even in the richer countries. About 40 years ago, while covering an FAO regional conference in Kingston, I interviewed a member of the US delegation who grew up during the rough time between the two world wars.

The president of the day, Herbert Hoover, preached thrift, and he said that as a child his household had what they called a "Hoover plate". It meant that he and his siblings had to eat everything they put on their plate, leaving it completely empty at the end of the meal. That resonated with me, as the same rule applied in our house—you could take as much as you wanted, but you had to eat all of it.

This is one phenomenon which doesn't need a crash programme, government legislation or campaign. We just have to remember, every day, our parents' exhortation to "think of the poor starving children in Africa" as we prepare to chuck perfectly good food into the garbage. "Waste not, want not" takes on a new, urgent meaning.

Canadians Believe the Global Food Crisis Will Worsen

Nicholas Hirst

Nicholas Hirst reports that, according to the National Farmers Union of Canada, grain supplies are at their lowest in decades, ocean fisheries are failing, global warming is causing crop failures, and single strain crops risk ruin from disease. Hirst argues that although it would be better for everyone to eat less meat and use less fossil fuel, it is difficult to deny developing countries the amenities that the Western world has long enjoyed. He predicts growing food shortages. Hirst is the CEO of Original Pictures, Inc., a Winnipeg-based television and film production company.

As you read, consider the following questions:

1. What fraction of the world's ocean fisheries have collapsed?
2. What crop disease has been caused by wet weather in North America?
3. According to Hirst, the production of ethanol addresses one shortage, but causes another. What are the two shortages to which Hirst refers?

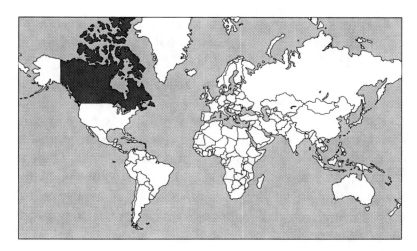

At the beginning of the summer [2007], the National Farmers Union [NFU] of Canada put out a press release that included the headline *Global food crisis emerging.*

The release is scary reading. Based on early predictions by the United States Department of Agriculture on world grain supply and demand for the 2007–08 crop year, the NFU's director of research, Darrin Qualman, broadcasts a dire warning that "we are in the opening phase of an intensifying food shortage."

Qualman means a worldwide shortage.

Despite the so-called "green revolution," the miracle of fertilizers, irrigation techniques, and disease-resistant grains, the world, once again is in danger of not feeding itself.

A Worldwide Food Shortage

As the world went into the Northern Hemisphere's summer, total grain supplies were the lowest in the 47 periods for which data exists and were quite possibly at their lowest levels in a century. This crop season would mark the seventh year out of the past eight in which global grain production fell short of demand.

"The world is consistently failing to produce as much grain as it uses," Qualman said.

Despite the so-called "green revolution," the miracle of fertilizers, irrigation techniques, and disease-resistant grains, the world, once again is in danger of not feeding itself. There are all kinds of reasons for this: population growth, climate change, a shift to feeding livestock instead of using grain directly for food, which is a less efficient way of feeding people, and growing demand for ethanol.

There are no easy solutions and there are other potential problems. The collapse of cod supplies is well-known, but many edible fish species are also in danger. Qualman says one-third of ocean fisheries are already in collapse and scientific journals estimate that two-thirds may be in collapse by 2025.

The warning signs are very real and much like climate change, the potential food shortage is a result of the way we consume and live our lives.

Increasing Crop Diseases

Climate change may exacerbate grain shortages. Global warming has been largely associated with drier conditions in grain-growing areas, but that is far from universal. Some areas in North America have been having unusually wet weather in spring—ideal conditions for scab, or head blight. Scab hit Nebraska wheat fields this year. The Broad Institute, a research body supported by the Massachusetts Institute of Technology, Harvard and affiliated hospitals warns that head blight "is becoming a threat to the world's food supply."

The Food and Agriculture Organization [FAO] of the United Nations reported earlier this year [2007] that a new

Environmental Degradation of the Oceans Impacts the Global Food Supply

The world's oceans are already under stress as a result of overfishing, pollution and other environmentally damaging activities in the coastal zones and now on the high seas.

Climate change is presenting a further and wide-ranging challenge with new and emerging threats to the sustainability and productivity of a key economic and environmental resource. . . .

The challenge of the seas and oceans in terms of monitoring has always been a formidable one with the terrestrial world more visible and easier to see. This is despite fisheries contributing to the global food supply and a supporter of livelihoods and cultures for millennia.

However, there is growing and abundant evidence that the rate of environmental degradation in the oceans may have progressed further than anything yet seen on land. . . .

[F]ishing grounds are increasingly damaged by over-harvesting, unsustainable bottom trawling and other fishing practices, pollution and dead zones, and a striking pattern of invasive species infestations in the same areas.

Achim Steiner, "Preface," In Dead Water, *United Nations Environment Program, 2008, p. 6.*

and virulent fungus of wheat-stem rust had spread from East Africa to Yemen. Some 80 per cent of wheat varieties in Africa and Asia are susceptible to the disease.

Crop diseases are nothing new. The Irish potato famine was caused by disease. The Bible is replete with stories of famine and the need to store grains.

Modern techniques have led to disease-resistant strains. Most strains of wheat rust in North America, for example, have been combatted by cultivation of resistant strains. Agriculturists, however, stress the need for cultivation of many varieties of all crops. A single strain is always vulnerable to a new, mutated form of any crop disease. The Irish potato famine was a result of over-reliance on one variety.

Famine Will First Affect the Poor

The world's food supplies may not be as robust as they were 20 years ago, nonetheless, we are not all about to starve. Famine, for the next little while at least, is going to affect others—the poorer nations of the Earth—not us.

It won't come to the West first, but that there's still every reason to be concerned. The warning signs are very real and much like climate change, the potential food shortage is a result of the way we consume and live our lives.

It's also an example of how solving one problem tends to produce another. The production of ethanol reduces dependence on oil, but diverts grains from the food supply, thereby assisting in one shortage but threatening another.

For the world's food supply, it would be better if we all ate less meat and got our proteins in a different way, but we are as used to our diet as we are to driving cars and taking airplanes and we are now using grain to do so. Having had the benefit, in the West, of eating what we want, it is hard now to deny developing countries the same, just as it is difficult to argue against their increasing use of fossil fuels when the West has caused the great majority of the greenhouse-gas effect so far.

The prospect of climate change has now gained widespread acceptance, although the response is less clear. The building danger of food shortages, however, as production plateaus and the world population continues to increase is less well appreciated and almost totally without political action.

Qualman of the NFU is not a scaremonger. He's telling it as it is. So here's a prediction: Food is the next big global news story and just like climate change it will generate huge controversy.

The problem can be ignored, but it won't go away.

China and India Are Causing the Global Food Crisis

Rüdiger Falksohn et al., translated from German by Christopher Sultan

Staff writer Rüdiger Falksohn and his colleagues at Spiegel, *a large German magazine, argue that China and India are placing extraordinary pressure on the world food supply as their populations demand more and better food at a time when arable land in both countries is decreasing. According to the writers, China has invested in South American and African farmland, moving large numbers of Chinese farmers there to produce food. Both countries are stockpiling food, and India has instituted export bans on rice. The* Spiegel *writers contend that speculators and profiteers are the ones benefiting from the Chinese and Indian strategies.*

As you read, consider the following questions:

1. What prompted farmers in South America to move into the Amazon basin to grow soybeans?
2. Why has it become difficult to import rice from Thailand, Indonesia and Vietnam?
3. How were many Indian farmers driven into ruin, according to the authors of this viewpoint?

Rüdiger Falksohn et al., "The Struggle to Satisfy China and India's Hunger," translated by Christopher Sultan, *Spiegel Online*, April 28, 2008. www.spiegel.de. © *Der Spiegel* 2008. All rights reserved. Reproduced by permission.

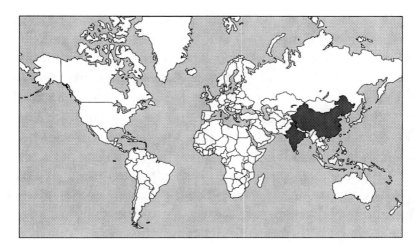

With their huge populations, China and India exert an unparalleled force on world food markets. They are looking abroad as it becomes more difficult for them to be self-sufficient—and the increasing demand often has disastrous consequences across the globe.

Santarém, in the heart of the Brazilian rainforest, is a modest little city. Quaint passenger steamers bob next to the breakwater of the Tapajós River, which flows into the Amazon here, while couples walk hand-in-hand along the riverfront.

The city would be even more idyllic, however, if the view of the cloudy tropical sky in the background were not marred by a terminal operated by the American agricultural conglomerate Cargill.

South American Soybeans Headed for China

The steel structure protrudes into the air like the neck of a giraffe, constantly spewing ton after ton of soybeans into the holds of waiting ships. Every hour, a giant freighter departs for the mouth of the Amazon, 600 kilometers (373 miles) away. From there, the ships will set sail for China.

Until the end of the last century, soybeans were practically unknown in the Amazon basin. It was not until the grain terminal was built that soybean farmers came to the region from farther south. The land there was cheaper, the banks were offering low-interest loans and sales to Cargill were guaranteed.

Villages, rubber plantations and grazing land for cattle were transformed into bean fields. The farmers cut enormous swathes into the rainforest, until environmentalists put a temporary stop to the unchecked rash of clearcutting. In Mato Grosso, the most important farming region, producers and environmental activists agreed on a two-year moratorium on the purchase of soybeans from the Amazon basin.

But now the moratorium is set to expire and prices are rising. This is mainly the result of China's thirst for raw materials, says Pedro Jacyr Bongiolo, the president of the André Maggi Group, one of the world's largest soybean producers.

From the Río de la Plata to the Amazon, the Chinese are sucking the markets for soybeans dry.

Soybean Production Causes Environmental Devastation

From the Río de la Plata to the Amazon, the Chinese are sucking the markets for soybeans dry. Large segments of the state of Mato Grosso are already covered with a green, pesticide-drenched monoculture. In the dry season between August and November, a cloud of smoke descends on Cuiabá, the capital of Mato Grosso. Despite a government ban, many farmers burn down sections of the rainforest to gain more farmland.

In neighboring Argentina, thick smoke even darkened the skies in the capital Buenos Aires two weeks ago. In that case, the smoke was coming from bush fires set by cattle ranchers in the nearby delta of the Paraná River. The ranchers need more pastureland because expanding soybean farms are swallowing up their traditional pastures. Here, too, the soybeans are being produced for the Chinese market.

It has long been clear who the losers are in this soybean rush. In Santarém, hundreds of small farmers became unemployed when they sold their fields to soybean farmers. The money was quickly spent, and now most of them live in slums, because there are now few jobs in agriculture.

China and India, faced with growing populations and shrinking agricultural land, are increasingly dependent on food imports from abroad.

"Soy is a culture of death," says union leader Ivete Bastos. But few are interested in opinions like hers, especially not 16,000 kilometers away in China. Brazil is one of China's major trading partners. Long-term contracts between the two countries are intended to secure raw materials for China—and, more recently, food products in particular.

The rising world power, with its population of 1.3 billion, must take steps to ensure that it too does not become a victim of the global food crisis, having only recently managed to win the fight against poverty for much of its population at home. But now India, home to 1.1 billion people, has caught up with China in terms of the power it wields as a massive market. Together, the two Asian nations must feed more than a third of the world's population. In times of exploding food prices, their sheer size alone makes the crisis even worse.

The Indians and Chinese Are Building Food Reserves

To confront this growing problem and because wheat production has stagnated since the turn of the millennium, India has recently decided to develop an additional strategic food reserve. Statisticians have calculated that the demand for food increases by 0.7 percent for each percentage point of Indian growth. According to this calculation, last year alone [2007], when India's per capita growth was about 7.5 percent, the country needed about 5.2 percent more food, especially more expensive non-staple foods. The situation is similar in China. Its global purchases of soybeans are a consequence of changes in eating habits. More than half of all soybean production in the world now ends up in China.

It isn't difficult to imagine what happens to prices when the world's two most populous countries buy up other food products in a similarly aggressive fashion. In more and more dangerously poor countries, wheat and meat have become an almost unaffordable luxury, while famine and hunger riots are only likely to get worse. London-based author Raj Patel, whose new book *Stuffed and Starved* takes a critical look at the global food industry, warns that the events in Haiti are "a sign of things to come."

A large share of the soybean harvest is traded at the Chicago Board of Trade. Although one is unlikely to find the Chinese there, they are the topic of many conversations. They sweep the market clean every day, "as if they had a giant broom," say traders. Chinese farmers need more and more feed for their livestock, while Chinese families are using more and more cooking oil.

The National Development and Reform Commission in Beijing is in charge of crisis management. It hopes to put a stop to spiraling prices by reducing import duties, but this hasn't worked as planned. A stampede even erupted at a supermarket in Chongqing, when customers rushed into the store to take advantage of a sale of cooking oil. Three people were trampled to death and 31 were injured.

Calming Panic in China

Chinese Prime Minister Wen Jiabao tried to console himself and his fellow Chinese when he said: "With grain in our hands

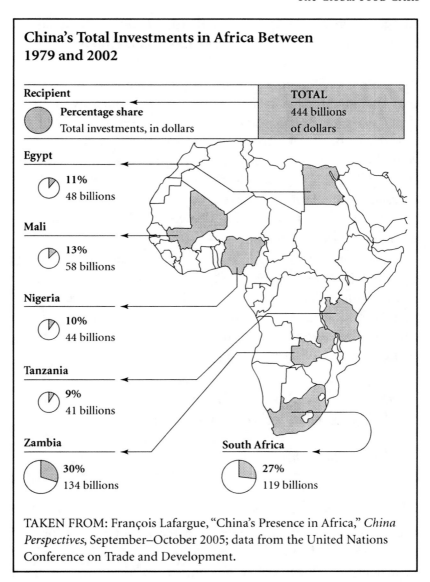

China's Total Investments in Africa Between 1979 and 2002

Recipient	TOTAL
⬤ Percentage share	444 billions
Total investments, in dollars	of dollars

Egypt
11%
48 billions

Mali
13%
58 billions

Nigeria
10%
44 billions

Tanzania
9%
41 billions

Zambia
30%
134 billions

South Africa
27%
119 billions

TAKEN FROM: François Lafargue, "China's Presence in Africa," *China Perspectives*, September–October 2005; data from the United Nations Conference on Trade and Development.

there is no need to panic." But the Chinese Communist Party has recently become concerned over the potential threat to calm and order posed by supply bottlenecks. Even in affluent Hong Kong, consumers bought up all the rice in stores in a collective attack of panic buying. To discourage such behavior, the government media have taken to constantly broadcasting images of lush fields and well-stocked supermarkets.

In an effort to restore calm, Wen says that China is able to meet most of its demand for rice from domestic supply, and that the government even has 40 to 50 million tons in emergency reserves. But there is still a gap between supply and demand of about 10 percent, which means that the country must import rice for 130 million people. This has become extremely difficult, because the key exporting nations, Thailand, Indonesia and Vietnam, have restricted their exports to prevent their supplies from being depleted by hoarders and their own people being left hungry.

Since January [2008], China has also blocked grain exports by imposing new duties. Using export quotas, subsidies for farmers and price controls, Beijing hopes to safeguard the domestic food supply. The government even monitors fields by satellite to prevent them from suddenly and illegally being turned into building land.

[Indian farmers] produce hardly any more grain than in the 1970s, when the country declared for the first time that it was self-sufficient. But India's population has doubled since then.

China Invests in Africa

But none of this can be effective in the long term. China and India, faced with growing populations and shrinking agricultural land, are increasingly dependent on food imports from abroad. Beijing has calculated that it needs 120 million hectares (296 million acres, or an area about the size of South Africa) of arable land to feed the country. The amount of land currently available for farming is only slightly above that figure, and fertile fields are disappearing beneath concrete daily.

And because almost all halfway fertile land is used for agriculture, the soil eventually becomes depleted of nutrients. China already consumes a third of world fertilizer production. This drives up prices, and at some point even fertilizer is no longer effective on over-farmed land.

"Most increases in productivity with such rudimentary means have already been exhausted," says Jonathan Anderson, an agricultural expert with Swiss bank UBS. In northern China, the soil is already so poor that the authorities have ordered farmers to keep their livestock in stalls to prevent further erosion of pastures and excessive rainwater runoff.

China is busy seeking solutions for all of these problems. Experts from the Trade Ministry have proposed that Chinese agricultural operations invest directly in Southeast Asia and Africa, where they could establish farms to satisfy the country's demand for grain. Although surplus harvests are a rarity in Africa, Chinese experts are already training local farmers in ways to improve their crop yields.

More than 10 years ago, Chinese farmers took over a dozen large farms in Zambia. They enjoy generous support from the government in the capital Lusaka, pay few taxes and are expected to bring innovation to and stimulate local agriculture.

In Uganda, the government of President Yoweri Museveni has provided 400 Chinese farmers with about 4,000 hectares (9,867 acres) of cropland. "We bring along experience and modern machinery," says an enthusiastic Liu Jianjun, the chairman of a Chinese-African economic alliance. "And we have high-quality seed that is far more productive than domestic varieties."

The Asians, who are by no means merely pursuing altruistic development objectives in Africa, hope that their efforts will eventually pay off. At home, new cities are swallowing up huge chunks of land, displacing millions of farmers. Indeed, it would suit China well if as many people as possible were to emigrate. There are already 750,000 Chinese working in Africa today.

The Situation in India

In contrast to China, India enacted market reforms in the 1990s that led to hundreds of thousands of farmers becoming dependent on multinational corporations. They were led to believe that genetic engineering would solve their problems and, as a result, many switched from food crops to useful plants like cotton. But the plants were susceptible to pests. In addition, the new crops required expensive special fertilizers and, in some cases, the purchase of new seeds every year. This drove tens of thousands into financial ruin and even suicide.

India is still a long way from overcoming acute poverty. Seventy percent of all Indians live in villages and remote hamlets, most of them in poverty. They produce hardly any more grain than in the 1970s, when the country declared for the first time that it was self-sufficient. But India's population has doubled since then.

Since January, food prices have risen by 40 percent in India, and inflation is at 7 percent. For Prime Minister Manmohan Singh, the situation is so dire that it poses an acute threat to his coalition government. The government subsidizes palm oil and imported grain, and grain futures transactions are prohibited. As a result, a hunger crisis is not to be expected for the time being.

Meanwhile, Maoist groups like the radical Naxalites have benefited for years from the plight of farmers, and have even established alternative administrations in a growing number of districts.

Trade Restrictions and Greed

India is also trying to secure food imports through bilateral agreements, with Kazakhstan, for example. In addition, the country plans to "invest heavily in Africa," as Prime Minister

Singh has said. Besides, politicians in New Delhi have been almost as quick to resort to trade restrictions as neighboring countries. In early March, they imposed a ban on exports of almost all types of rice. As a result, the current harvest, one of the best in years, is being kept off the world market. Rice, the most important staple food for about 4 billion people in Africa and Asia, is already selling for more than $1,000 a ton in some cases.

Speculators and major producers are the ones who are currently benefiting the most from new conditions in the marketplace: from the reduction in supply caused by export bans, from the feverish hoarding of available products and from the changes in India and China that are increasingly shaping the global market. And there is no solution to these problems in sight.

Now that rice has become so expensive, it has aroused completely new kinds of greed. In Thailand, for example, the crop is disappearing from fields.

The thieves, who come under the cover of night, are thorough. A farmer in Sing Buri Province, for example, arrived at his rice field early one morning to find that the entire field had been harvested. It must have been the work of a team, and they must have used tractors, he says. "When the prices are low, we don't make enough money, and when they are high we get robbed," he complains.

As a last resort against rice thieves in Sing Bud, farmers have taken matters into their own hands. Some recently started spending nights keeping watch on their fields—to ward off local profiteers of the worldwide food crisis in person.

A New Zealand Perspective on the Global Food Crisis

Barry Coates

Barry Coates counters the argument that the world food crisis can be solved with new technology, asserting that millions of people are on the brink of starvation. He attributes riots around the world to food shortages, and argues that the food crisis must be used to institute new reforms to help poor people worldwide. Coates also contends that the world must stop the rush to biofuels and that international action is necessary to help developing countries cope with climate change. Coates is the executive director of Oxfam New Zealand, an international aid agency.

As you read, consider the following questions:

1. How much money do people in Africa, Asia, the Middle East, and Latin American spend on food?
2. How many countries does the World Bank believe face social unrest due to high food costs?
3. How should the food aid system be improved, according to Coates?

Garth George [a columnist for the *New Zealand Herald*] says he has read all about the food crisis but remains unconcerned. He suggests we can develop new methods of food

Barry Coates, "A Hungry World Is An Angry World," *New Zealand Herald*, May 6, 2008, p. 11. Copyright 2008 Independent News & Meida PLC. Reproduced by permission.

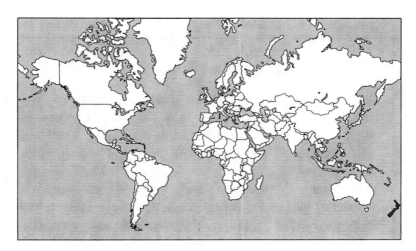

production before parts of the world face starvation. Wrong. Large numbers of people are already starving. Surely we are concerned about that.

Tonight, more than 850 million people will go to bed hungry. Tomorrow won't be any better. Hunger is already a leading cause of death worldwide, killing an estimated 10 million people every year—more than AIDS, tuberculosis and malaria combined.

In Africa, Asia, the Middle East and Latin America, many people already spend 80 cents of every dollar they earn on food. The impact of recent record highs in prices of rice, corn, and wheat on these people—the world's poorest—is becoming increasingly clear.

Estimates by the Asian Development Bank put 300 million people in India, Bangladesh and Pakistan alone at risk of starvation due to the rising prices. In Senegal [in western Africa], Oxfam staff have seen evidence that the usual "lean season" is coming on earlier as a result of price rises.

There are lower stocks in markets that usually have surpluses at this time of year, and people are eating alternative food and selling their animals already.

Despair Becomes Violence

Should we be surprised that despair often turns into violence? The food crisis afflicts the world's poor—in Africa, South Asia and the Middle East—like a biblical plague. Prices for staples like rice, corn and wheat, which were relatively stable for years, have skyrocketed by over 180 percent in the last three years. A bottleneck is developing whose consequences are potentially more severe than the global crisis in the financial markets. With nothing left to lose, people on the brink of starvation are more likely to react with boundless fury.

Spiegel, *"The Fury of the Poor,"*
April 14, 2008. www.spiegel.de.

Senegalese pastoralists are buying food earlier than usual and Mauritanian herders are coming over the border in search of pasture. This is having a direct impact on livelihoods and there is increased tension between different groups for natural resources, and an increase in banditry.

Rising Food Prices Cause Social Unrest

The World Bank is now [May 2008] warning that 33 countries face potential social unrest because of the huge hike in food and energy prices. Food riots have already broken out in countries such as Egypt, Tanzania and Mexico as people get hungrier.

A perfect storm of factors has caused prices to rise to unprecedented levels over a very short period of time. Climate change is causing increasingly erratic weather—bigger floods, and more severe droughts—which is destroying or damaging crops and reducing supply.

Higher oil and energy prices are increasing the cost of inputs like fertiliser while transport costs soar because of expensive fuel. Demand for biofuels—energy made from crops like corn and sugar—means that hungry people are competing with hungry cars for the same output.

Growing populations in India and China are eating more meat—which requires huge quantities of grain for animal feed. Finally, speculation on commodity markets, encouraged by high prices, is further upping the pressure.

Scientists warn that climate change could reduce African agriculture productivity by as much as 20–30 per cent.

Overdue Reforms

The current situation presents a huge threat to poor people and to agencies like Oxfam who are working to help them, but it must also be used as an opportunity to bring long overdue reforms that will help poor people in developing countries in the long-term.

Most of the world's poorest people make a living from agriculture, so higher prices could offer the possibility of a better livelihood. Structural problems such as under-investment in agriculture and unfair trade rules must be addressed. While quick to criticise export bans by developing countries, the EU [European Union], US [United States] and World Bank have failed to own up to their own contributions to the food crisis. Trade-distorting export agricultural subsidies and the dumping of surplus crops have increased poor countries' dependence on food imports. Decades of trade liberalization have deprived developing countries of the policy tools to respond to the problem, with export bans remaining as one of the few options poor countries have.

Ending the Rush to Biofuels

We must end the headlong rush towards more biofuels, which is having a negative impact on poor people and the environment and contributing to price rises. As scientists warn that climate change could reduce African agriculture productivity by as much as 20–30 per cent, we must take urgent international action to reduce carbon emissions and to help poor countries adapt to the impacts of global climate change.

Finally, although food aid is important, the system needs improving. Instead of dumping surplus as "in kind" food aid, donors should provide cash for governments and aid agencies to buy locally. This is more efficient and better for local agriculture.

Garth George is right—while our groceries may be costing us more than they did a year ago, we are lucky to be living in a land of plenty. But this is no reason to stop thinking and acting globally. We must remember that even without the current food crisis, over 850 million people do not have enough to eat. Now many more face a similar fate.

Mass starvation is completely avoidable.

Periodical Bibliography

The following articles have been selected to supplement the diverse views presented in this chapter.

Anthony Faiola "Worldwide, Feast Becomes Famine: In the Midst of a Global Shortage of Grains, Food Prices Are Soaring, Threatening the Most Vulnerable," *The Sunday Independent* (South Africa), May 4, 2008.

Rick Hampson "Ethiopia's New Famine: 'A Ticking Time Bomb,'" *USA Today*, August 17, 2008.

Teodros Kiros "The Causes of Famine," *Ethiopian Online Newsletter*, March 6, 2006. www.dekialula.com.

Kyodo News International (Tokyo, Japan) "U.N. Food Summit Opens to Address Food Crisis," June 4, 2008.

George Monbiot "Comment & Debate: Population Growth Is a Threat," *The Guardian*, January 29, 2008.

Joyce Mulama "People Are Not Starving Because of a Lack of Food," Africa News Service, March 16, 2006.

Moyiga Nduru "Africa: Two Decades After Famine, Ethiopians Still Go Hungry," Inter Press Service News Agency, March 20, 2007.

Stefan Steinberg "Financial Speculators Reap Profits from Global Hunger," Global Research, April 24, 2008.

C. Peter Timmer "Japan Ducks Rice-Crisis Solution," *Asia Times*, July 18, 2008.

John Vidal "Food Crisis Looms with Climate Change," *Manila Bulletin*, November 4, 2007.

Jonathan Watts "Global Food Crisis: More Wealth, More Meat. How China's Rise Spells Trouble," *The Guardian*, May 30, 2008.

 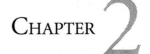

CHAPTER 2

Famine and Natural Disasters

Africa Experiences Famine Due to Drought

Peter Mwaura

Peter Mwaura asserts that famine is more devastating to African countries than to countries in other continents. Further, he states that drought is the single worst natural disaster on the African continent in terms of economic loss and deaths. African nations are more vulnerable to drought-related disaster because of the widespread poverty of the drylands regions. Governmental and world failure to address poverty in the drylands, Mwaura argues, puts African people and nations at great risk. Mwaura is a Kenyan journalist who writes for the Daily Nation.

As you read, consider the following questions:

1. What national leader was overthrown as a result of famine in Ethiopia in 1984–1985?
2. How many deaths per year can be attributed to drought in Indonesia? In Australia?
3. Who are some of the disadvantaged groups found in Africa's drylands?

In recent years drought-related famine has killed more people in Africa than in any other continent even though it is only the second driest after Asia.

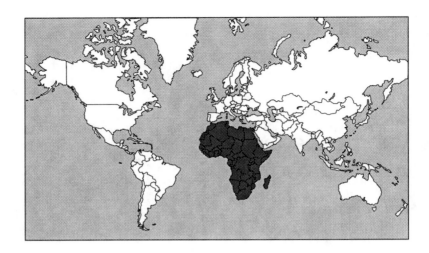

Since the Sahelian drought of 1973–74 and Ethiopian famine of 1984–85, drought and famine have been associated in peoples' minds with Africa.

The Sahelian drought, which affected the semi-arid zone that extended from northern Senegal in the west to eastern Sudan and parts of Ethiopia, marked the beginning of food aid to Africa. The Ethiopian famine, in which an estimated one million people died and Emperor Halle Selassie was overthrown, provoked an international appeal. Irish musician Bob Geldof launched Band Aid and American star musicians recorded the smash hit song "We Are the World, We Are the Children"—which helped raise more than $60 million for the famine victims.

In Africa drought is the single most important natural hazard in terms of shattered livelihoods, starvation, deaths, and nutrition-related diseases.

African countries are easily devastated by droughts. Drylands cover 43 per cent of Africa's land surface and drought is considered a normal fact of life. According to a study by the United Nations Development Programme (UNDP), while drought occurs in all continents, seven out of the 10 most vulnerable countries are in Africa (Somalia, Sudan, Ethiopia, Uganda, Chad, Mauritania and Mozambique).

Drought Is a Continental Natural Disaster

In Africa drought is the single most important natural hazard in terms of shattered livelihoods, starvation, deaths, and nutrition-related diseases. According to the UNDP study, the effects of drought are "insidious" due to their "creeping nature." Deaths are simply the end result of a ravaging process.

During the drought in the early 1970s, 1980s, the beginning of the 1990s and 2001 some 50 million Africans were affected. During the 1980–2000 period tens of thousands died in just three countries—Ethiopia, Sudan and Mozambique.

Drought in Africa causes economic losses of tens of millions of dollars and can reverse national development gains of several years. The crushing impacts are much greater for the poor people.

Countries with economies that are relatively simple and predominantly agricultural suffer most under drought conditions. In such countries the effect of drought increases their balance of trade deficits, donor and food aid dependency, urban migration of poor people, and the costs of service provision and welfare.

In countries such as South Africa whose economies are considered intermediate, the impacts of drought are better absorbed by a more complex and diversified economy. Similarly, in mineral-exporting countries such as Botswana and Namibia the impacts are cushioned by the mineral sectors of the economy, which are de-linked from the rainfall-dependent sectors.

Drought Can Destroy Economic Development

In many countries the frequency, duration and severity of drought can have significant impact on the Gross Domestic

Africa Is at the Greatest Risk of Drought Mortality

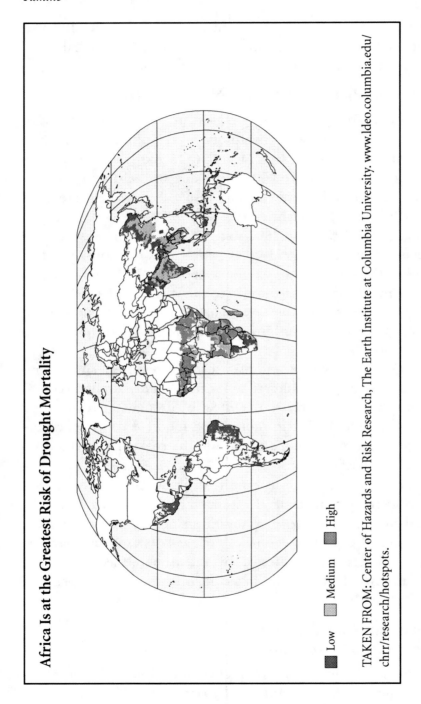

Low Medium High

TAKEN FROM: Center of Hazards and Risk Research, The Earth Institute at Columbia University. www.ldeo.columbia.edu/chrr/research/hotspots.

Product (GDP) and reverse many apparently unrelated investments in national development. Drought in a simple or intermediate economy can have a particularly significant impact on the economy both directly and through knock-on effects.

For example, the 1990–91 drought in Zimbabwe resulted in a 45 per cent drop in national agricultural production, 62 per cent in stock market, nine per cent in manufacturing output and one per cent in GDP. The 1999–2001 drought in Kenya cost the economy some Sh180 billion. As a proportion of the national economy, this figure is a very significant loss and can best be thought of as foregone development, for example, in roads, schools and hospitals not built.

Drought in an African country . . . may cause major human suffering including death, whilst a drought of a similar severity in an American, or even in an Asian country, only has an economic impact.

A worldwide survey of drought-prone societies by UNDP reveals that the way countries manage the risk of drought depends partly on their levels of economic development. The study found a very high inverse correlation between the Gross National Product (GNP) and human mortality in the face of drought.

Wealthy Countries Can Survive Drought While Poor Countries Cannot

Most of the human fatalities from drought and related disasters are experienced in the developing countries, while developed countries record only economic losses that are easily absorbed by their larger economies. Drought in an African country, say Malawi or Mozambique, may cause major human suffering including death, whilst a drought of a similar severity in an American, or even in an Asian country, only has an economic impact.

For example, the drought of 1988 in the United States of America caused an estimated damage of $40 billion due to direct and knock-on effects on the economy. The size of the US economy was sufficient to absorb this shock. An African country with a simple agricultural economy would almost certainly have gone under.

The effects of a natural hazard like drought are mediated through a socio-economic system, which either attenuates or exacerbates the natural effects, according to a recent UNDP report. For example in Indonesia, which has the same drought exposure as Australia, some 25,000 deaths per year were attributed to drought, whereas in Australia there were none. India has more regularly hungry people than all of Africa put together, but virtually nobody starves in India and the country does not depend on foreign aid. India, in fact, has a wheat surplus from year to year.

During the 1980–2000 exposure to drought in several countries across the globe there were no drought-related deaths in Bolivia, Jordan, Ecuador, Spain and the United States while there were thousands of deaths in Ethiopia, Sudan, Mozambique, Chad, Somalia and Mauritania.

Africa Has Not Addressed Drought Adequately

Why is Africa in such a perilous position? The scientific knowledge exists that could enable the continent [to] reduce its vulnerability to drought. In his message to the world on the World Water 2004, UN Secretary General Kofi Annan said that modern society has distinct advantages over those civilizations of the past that suffered or even collapsed for reasons linked to water.

"We have great knowledge, and the capacity to disperse that knowledge to the remotest places on earth. We are also beneficiaries of scientific leaps that have improved weather forecasting, agricultural practices, natural resources management, disaster prevention, preparedness and management," he said.

But only a rational and informed political, social and cultural response—and public participation in all stages of the disaster management cycle—can reduce disaster vulnerability, and ensure that hazards do not turn into unmanageable disasters.

Africa has not benefited from this scientific knowledge, or rather it has not taken a "rational and informed political, social and cultural response" to reduce disaster vulnerability and ensure that hazards do not turn into unmanageable disasters. Africa has not adopted the right policies to combat the impacts of drought. That is why many analysts say that most famines in Africa are policy, not meteorological, famines.

Factors such as inappropriate land tenure, poor infrastructure and provision of services can exacerbate the effects of drought. . . . Africa is badly governed and many of the famines in Africa are policy famines.

A number of international organisations exist to help countries cope with drought. The Food and Agriculture Organisation (FAO) operates a global information and early warning system, while UNDP has a unit dedicated to assisting countries to drought-proof their societies.

UNDP's Drylands Development Centre, which is located in Nairobi, addresses the question of drought-related vulnerability through policy reform. For example, it has embarked on a project to help southern African countries enhancing their resilience to drought.

Africa is lagging behind in drought-proofing because of a number of factors. Eric Patrick, a policy specialist with the Drylands Development Centre, lists some of the factors that increase or decrease vulnerability to drought.

83

Factors That Increase Vulnerability to Drought

First, there are the patterns taken by drought, which are exacerbated by conflict and competition for resources, creating a vicious circle. This is well illustrated in northern Kenya and the greater Horn of Africa, where conflict has engulfed the region, thus amplifying the impacts of drought.

Second, there are dysfunctional socio-economic systems, which may magnify the natural impacts of drought. Factors such as inappropriate land tenure, poor infrastructure and provision of services can exacerbate the effects of drought. This is another way of saying that Africa is badly governed and many of the famines in Africa are policy famines.

Third, there is the feeling that the government can always turn to humanitarian aid to bail it from a famine situation. The international system for "humanitarian dumping" of surplus grains insures Africa against the vagaries of nature and insulates many African leaders from the political fallout of bad policies that perpetuate food insecurity.

A close look at Africa's vulnerability to drought shows that poverty is in fact the root cause. African drylands are characterised by endemic poverty.

For example, in Cameroon although 31 per cent of the population live in the semi-arid Northern Region, 50 per cent of the country's poorest people are found there; they have the highest rates of illiteracy, poor housing and maternal mortality. Similarly, in Kenya the highest incidence of poverty is in its northern arid and semi-arid districts, where life expectancy, adult literacy, secondary school enrollment are lower than in other areas.

Within Africa's drylands are found many disadvantaged groups, such as female-headed households, land-poor farmers, and pastoralists who have no control on external factors that impact on their livelihoods.

The Special Challenges of Drylands

Africa's drylands face special challenges that are not generally found in other areas and they have fallen behind in development. There is a risk that the gap in development will widen in [the] future unless there is a change in thinking and strategies.

More often than not Africa's drylands do not receive the attention they deserve in terms of resource allocation and development attention. And when they receive such attention it is usually inappropriate, unsustainable or not fully backed up with the right resources or management skills.

According to a UNDP report, low financial rates of return, financial unsustainability, mismanagement and unforeseen consequences contribute to the poor project performance in Africa's drylands. Recent projects have tried to correct such mistakes but it is still generally held that dryland development projects are doomed to fail.

However, treating Africa's drylands as "development sinks" may be more expensive in lost production, food aid and social instability, according to the UNDP report. African countries must integrate drought into national development and mainstream drought risk in their decisions on development policies to free themselves from the consequences of recurring droughts.

In the Horn of Africa, Drought, Conflict, and Famine Are Linked

Meedan Mekonnen

Meedan Mekonnen examines the connections among conflict, drought and famine. She argues that drought can cause conflict as people fight over diminishing food and water supplies. She also asserts that although conflict does not cause drought, it does cause drought-related famine by making it difficult to move supplies to needy people. Mekonnen asserts that because drought, conflict, and famine are so closely entwined, suggested solutions must address all three problems. Mekonnen is from Ethiopia, and is a 2007 graduate of the Joan B. Kroc Institute for International Peace Studies at Notre Dame University, in South Bend, Indiana.

As you read, consider the following questions:

1. What are the natural causes of drought?

2. What country collapsed as a result of drought and famine in the early 1990s?

3. What are three key aspects of drought response, according the Mekonnen?

Meedan Mekonnen, "Drought, Famine, and Conflict: Case from the Horn of Africa," *Beyond Intractability*, September 2006. www.beyondintractability.org Copyright © 2003–2006 The Beyond Intractability Project. Reproduced by permission.

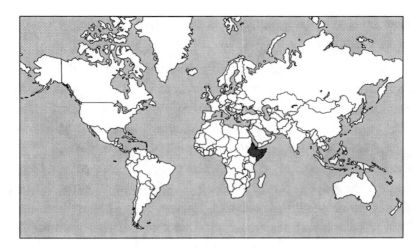

It is a shame that in the twenty-first century, a century heralded by great advances in technology and developed economies, that drought and famine still persists in some parts of the world. The end of the Cold War increased the hope of many people that the world's political and economic system would be changed for better, following the narrowing of ideological differences that had so polarized the world. It was hoped that humanity would be better off, as everyone benefited from a new era of world peace and economic development.

Conflict cannot change weather patterns, but it can affect agricultural practices, land use, and other social factors that intensify the effects of diminished rainfall, particularly by causing famine.

However, this has not been the case. On a daily basis, the international mass media is awash with reports of various conflicts across the world. At the same time, there is much news coverage of drought situations in various parts of the globe.

The Linkage of Drought, Famine, and Conflict

In the Horn of Africa especially, drought is part and parcel of daily life. It is so common that in many African societies, the drought season marks an important part of the annual calendar. In a recent BBC [British Broadcasting Corporation] report, the UN [United Nations] expressed fears that . . . "The world is in danger of allowing a drought in East Africa to become a humanitarian catastrophe". At the same time, I came across news headline that said, "Kenya drought worsens conflict." These headlines made me think more deeply about the two issues: if conflict and drought are the scourge of our modern world, it would therefore be appropriate to question their symbiotic relationship. If they are related, how do they influence each other? Is drought a cause of conflict or is conflict a cause of drought? Will drought always trigger conflict? Will conflict exacerbate drought? (Conflict cannot change weather patterns, but it can affect agricultural practices, land use, and other social factors that intensify the effects of diminished rainfall, particularly by causing famine). . . .

Drought is mainly a natural phenomenon that affects parts of the world. Some areas of the world with strong economies and viable political structures have successfully responded to the advent of drought in their countries by adjusting water storage, allocation, and usage patterns, while other parts of the world have dismally failed to do so. Africa is an example of an area that suffers from recurring drought and desertification. Short-lived droughts are seldom dangerous; but sequential drought years are. Though sequential droughts are common in the Horn of Africa, people there have not successfully responded to it; rather they have been devastated by it. Is this because almost all of the recent droughts and famines in the Horn of Africa region have occurred in situations of armed conflicts? A relationship seems likely. . . .

A Deadly Relationship: Drought, Conflict, and Famine

Drought:

Lack of rain means little water for crops, livestock and humans.

Conflict:

Competing groups fight for rapidly diminishing resources in drought-stricken areas. Conflict prevents the distribution of food aid as famine deepens, leading to more deaths.

Famine:

Insufficient food and water causes death.

Famine may be caused by drought, conflict, or both.

Source: Complied by editor.

I argue that drought is a contributing factor to conflict and conflict exacerbates drought, making famine more likely. Therefore, drought, conflict, and famine are inextricably linked, with each acting as a catalyst to the other. The situation in the Horn of Africa will be a showcase to support the thesis.

Definitions of Drought

Drought is a period of aridity, particularly when protracted, that causes widespread harm to crops or prevents their successful growth. Insufficient rainfall and unfavorable weather conditions are natural causes of drought. Environmental degradation caused by the overuse of farmland and deforestation—cutting of trees for household and other purposes— aggravate drought. People's lack of capacity to respond to

89

natural disasters and inefficient or lack of early warning systems also worsens the effects of drought.

Famine is often associated with drought. Different scholars have given various definitions of famine. [Indian economist] Amartya Sen defines famine as "unequal distribution of food supply." His argument is that famine is not a shortage of aggregate food supply, but the inability of individuals to afford available food. In this sense, a good harvest throughout a year does not guarantee that there will be no famine. In some instances, for example, governments have manipulated the food supply for political reasons, using food as a weapon.

People are dying from starvation, and they are also dying from conflict, as they fight for water and food.

[Anthropologist Alex] De Waal has another definition of famine that is drawn from a local perception of famine in Western Sudan. Famine, he says, is "a disruption of life, involving hunger and destitution and sometimes, [but] not always death." De Waal has tried to make a distinction between the European perception of famine—starvation to death—and the African view that says that famine involves hunger and destitution, but not necessarily death. Other scholars relate behavioral changes with famine. [Writer Jenny] Edkins, for example, states that famine is "a socio-economic process that causes the accelerated destitution of the most vulnerable and marginal groups in society." Trying to bring all these ideas together, I suggest that . . . a working definition of famine is a phenomenon in which a large percentage of population is so undernourished that death by starvation becomes very common.

Drought, prolonged conflict and regional instability, mismanagement of food supplies, and policy failures are causes of famine. In many cases, these situations exist together, each reinforcing each other

Drought Causes Conflict

Drought is one of the causes of conflict. Many areas affected by drought are arid and semiarid areas. Under normal circumstances, these areas are low in resources and under substantial ecological pressure. When drought occurs in such arid areas, the living conditions of local people become very difficult. In these conditions, the land yields no crops and water is insufficient for human consumption as well. People compete for the meager available resources. Pastoral communities are an example of this. Pastoralists depend on their livestock (camels, cattle, sheep, and goats) and move from place to place with their livestock to look for usable pasture land and water. During drought, their movement increases. Sometimes, different pastoral groups move to the same place and want to use the same scarce resources, which cause conflicts between the two communities. There is a history of pastoral communities fighting for scarce resources in Southern parts of Ethiopia, Northern Kenya, parts of Somalia and the Sudan. Most of the conflicts in those areas were manageable, and tend to be resolved by elderly leaders through traditional conflict resolution mechanisms on an ad hoc basis. However, these conflicts are exacerbated and more difficult to resolve when drought occurs.

The present conflict in Turkana in Northern Kenya is a case in point. The region is badly affected by drought. According to a recent [United Nations] World Food Programme [WFP] report, 3.5 million people are currently affected. People there are fighting for scarce resources. Oxfam [an international relief agency], which has a food program in the region, told the BBC that the drought had worsened the conflict there. People are dying from starvation, and they are also dying from conflict, as they fight for water and food. Families are losing their livestock, which is their main source of livelihood. Subsequently, drought-affected people migrate into other parts of the country. This spreads the pressure on resources and results in conflict spreading into other areas as well. In addition, nomadic groups take their cattle to farmlands in search of pasture. Often there is a conflict between farmers and cattle herders, a situation that is still happening in Northern Kenya and Southern Ethiopia.

Similarly, when the State of Somalia collapsed in early 1990s, the country was also suffering from drought and human caused famine. Rival pastoral clans who had been deprived of development investment invaded the fertile Juba River farming area. Many farmers were caught unprepared and they bore the brunt of the fighting.

The availability of small arms and light weapons along border areas where pastoral communities reside also contributes greatly to conflict. Arms ownership is regarded as necessary for the protection of one's community and livelihood in such areas, as they are situated in remote regions, far from the protection of regular state security. But the prevalence of arms also means the prevalence of armed conflict.

Governmental Response to Drought Can Fuel Conflict

The response of the central government to the drought-affected region determines, to some extent, when and where conflict breaks out. Delays of aid often create a feeling of alienation and marginalization among the affected groups. These communities may form different factions and rebel groups to address their frustration with the central government. In such contexts, conflict erupts among the rebel groups and between the rebels and the government in power.

For example, drought-caused famine was part of the cause of the Sudanese conflict. The Khartoum government was silent when the southern part of Sudan was hit by drought and famine. This angered the Southern people and strengthened their opposition to the Khartoum government. Similarly, the Ethiopian revolution of 1974 and the replacement of authoritarian rule was exacerbated by the monarchy's clumsy handling of famine in the northern part of that country. Likewise, while 8 million Ethiopian people were at risk of drought in 2000, Ethiopia and Eritrea were waging war. According to one BBC report, "War and drought are the two words forever associated with the Horn of Africa." This suggests that drought and conflict always reinforce each other or are two sides of a coin.

People at refugee settlement areas are exceptionally susceptible to famine. Relief aid is sometimes looted by rival groups which make humanitarian assistance additionally difficult.

Conflict Can Cause Famine

By the same token, conflict has been a contributing factor to drought-led famine. A government that engages in armed conflict has a high military expenditure. Shifting scarce resources to the military budget always weakens critical development needs of a country. When the government's full attention is on the conflict; they cannot pursue drought-relief, social, or development programs. In addition, the government usually spends all the available resources on the conflict, which also prevents it from addressing the economic needs of its people. Such a situation leads to famine. Poor communities are especially exposed to drought and famine since they lack the capacity to respond to natural disasters. Furthermore, when either the government or the rebels recruit soldiers that means taking productive labor from the individual households.

Landmines are an additional serious problem that has a profound impact on health, the economy, and the environment. In many war-torn countries these weapons have been scattered in farm fields, roads, even around schools and health centers. According to Adopt a Minefield, a UK-based organization, more than 80% of landmine causalities are civilians. Every day women and children are killed by landmines or injured during and after violent conflicts. Besides causing death and injury, landmines prevent people from using their farmlands and they block roads needed to fetch water. Landmines additionally cause village markets to close and communication between different villages to stop. Therefore, people either starve to death or wait for relief aid. But aid is also hampered or blocked entirely by mines in the roads. The Horn of African countries have been infested by landmines. For example, a UN Mine Action center survey indicated that the rural and nomadic people in Ethiopia and Eritrea are highly affected by landmines and unexploded ordinance [ammunition] left from long-lasting struggle of Eritrea for independence, Ethiopia's conflict with neighboring countries and the recent conflict between Ethiopia and Eritrea. The report states that there are around 6,295 victims of mine accidents in those two countries. Making the land safe and available for farming and grazing is even more challenging. This is yet another way in which armed conflict intensifies the effects of drought and causes famine.

Running away from conflict and persecution, leaving their home and land, many people become refugees in neighboring countries. According to a 2004 UNHCR [United Nations High Commissioner for Refugees] report the total number of refugees reached to 9.2 million in the world. Food aid, health care and human rights protection are the basic needs of refugees. Often it is beyond the capacity of host countries to provide such assistance. It even becomes challenging to humanitarian organizations and UNHCR. Hence, people at refugee settlement areas are exceptionally susceptible to famine. Relief aid is sometimes looted by rival groups which make humanitarian assistance additionally difficult. For instance, in the early 1990s in Somalia, fighting and looting made providing humanitarian assistance very difficult. As a result, many people died from famine, unable to obtain aid.

Attempted Solutions

If drought contributes to conflict and conflict has the potential to cause famine, what attempts have been done to address the problem? What mechanisms have been developed? How are such efforts integrated with peacebuilding?

One response to the problem of drought and famine was IGAD, the Intergovernmental Authority on Development. IGAD is a regional grouping of the Horn-Eastern African Countries of Djibouti, Eritrea, Ethiopia, Kenya, Somalia, Sudan and Uganda. It has its head office in Djibouti. It was established in 1986 by heads of the member states with a narrow mandate to address the severe drought and other natural disasters that caused widespread famine in the region. Initially, as a result of its limited role and focused program area, IGAD did not address conflict and related issues. In addition, some organizational and structural problems made the organization ineffective.

Yet the many conflicts in the region made efforts to address the problems of drought and famine more difficult. Internal conflicts in Sudan, the secession of Eritrea from Ethiopia, the civil war that led to the collapse of Somalia and other conflicts around border areas among neighboring countries all contributed to suffering and famine. Establishing an organization that could address the conflicts of the region was very vital. Although the former IGAD served as a forum for states to discuss issues related to drought, no state has dared to raise the question of resolving conflicts or differences.

In 1995 the heads of member States and governments decided to rejuvenate the organization into a regional political, economic, security, trade and development entity. At a regional summit in 1996, council ministers endorsed a plan to enhance regional cooperation in the areas of conflict prevention, management and resolution, humanitarian affairs, food security, environmental protection, and economic cooperation and integration. The organization's name officially changed to IGAD.

The presence and potentially threatening inter- and intrastate, communal and clan-based conflicts in the region were the main reasons that forced member states to expand IGAD's vision and mission. IGAD has been successful in mediating the Sudanese conflict, which resulted in the signing of a Comprehensive Peace Agreement in 2005 between the Sudanese government and the Southern People's Libration Army (SPLA). In addition, IGAD was involved in initiating the Somalia peace talks which later were able to provide a framework for a five-year transitional government in Somalia.

The Conflict Early Warning and Response System

The Conflict Early Warning and Response (CEWARN) Mechanism was born out of the new IGAD in 2002. Its objectives are to:

- support member states to prevent cross border pastoral conflicts,

- enable local communities to play an important role in preventing violent conflicts,

- enable the IGAD secretariat to pursue conflict prevention initiatives and

- provide members technical and financial support (IGAD). So far through CEWARN, IGAD is working on capacity-building and awareness about early warning signs of conflict.

Since 2004, IGAD has developed a project that targets pastoral communities of southwestern Ethiopia, northwestern Kenya, southeastern Sudan and northeastern Uganda that is named the Karamoja Cluster. Armed conflict in the cluster is increasing tremendously. According to baseline reports of CEWARN, adverse climatic conditions have been aggravated by violent incidents in the area. Further, the crisis caused unusual migratory movements of people and ongoing competition for scare resources. Interestingly, CEWARN mentioned that some peace initiatives are underway. However, none have succeeded, and the conflict has renewed. Apart from analyzing the Karamoja conflict, CEWARN has made recommendations to responsible bodies that include the local communities and respective governments. The CEWARN project again illustrates the argument that there is a direct relationship between drought and conflict and it is impossible to solve one problem without addressing both.

Drought, famine, and conflict are highly interlinked. None of the problems can be solved without addressing the others.

What Should Be Done?

Drought, famine, and conflict are highly interlinked. None of the problems can be solved without addressing the others.

Key aspects of drought response include:

1. Build an Early Warning System

   Developing a strong early warning system for drought and desertification is crucial. It should be adopted at local, national, and regional levels.

2. Strengthen Intergovernmental Cooperation

   States should strengthen cooperation among neighboring countries to combat drought and prevent conflicts. Furthermore, building networks and collaboration with various actors in the area helps to tackle problems of drought and conflict. For instance, the UN Convention to Combat Desertification has recommended research on "drought and desertification, identifying causal factors both natural and human, addressing specific needs of local populations and enhancing local knowledge, skills, and know how." This, they say, is an important area of collaboration.

3. Add Greater Capacity and Preparation to Traditional Mechanisms

Building the capacity and preparation of traditional mechanisms for combating drought is a third key factor. Some of the traditional mechanisms are collecting/ harvesting rainwater in man-made ponds, diversifying grazing lands, and planting trees such as cassava that adapt to dry climates. In addition, strengthening and empowering traditional conflict resolving mechanisms contribute to building relationships among and across communities, which diminishes the frequency and intensity of armed conflict, and encourages cooperative solutions to other problems—for instance, drought and famine.

Southern Africa Faces Famine Caused by Floods

Kitsepile Nyathi

Kitsepile Nyathi reports that unusual rainfall in southern Africa has caused terrible flooding that will inevitably lead to famine. The problem in Zimbabwe, the author asserts, is especially bad because the country is in its worst economic crisis in decades. The floods have not only wiped out crops and destroyed power grids, they have also leached out nutrients from the soil, coming at a time when there is an extreme fertilizer shortage, according to Nyathi. Nyathi is an African journalist who writes for Kenya Today *and* Daily Nation *newspapers.*

As you read, consider the following questions:

1. How many people have been displaced by floods in Mozambique and Zimbabwe, according to statistics from relief agencies?

2. Why is the commercial farming industry in Zimbabwe nearly non-existent, according to Nyathi?

3. According to Nyathi, why is Zimbabwe unable to import spare parts to repair its electrical equipment?

Kitsepile Nyathi, "Famine Looms as Southern Africa Faces Famine Caused by Floods," *Kenya Today*, January 23, 2008. www.politics.nationmedia.com. © Nation Media Group Limited, 2004. Reproduced by permission.

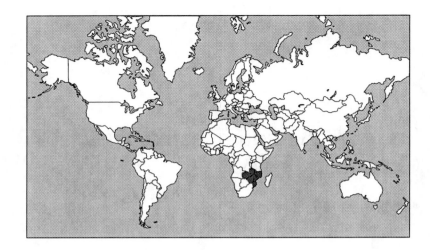

In Zimbabwe it was dubbed the "Mother of all Agricultural Seasons", amid high hopes that a normal rainy season would reverse almost 10 years of decline in agricultural productivity, which has spawned unending food shortages and an economic recession.

But after almost two months of torrential rainfall, Southern Africa is once again facing another failed cropping season, that will worsen food security in some countries, analysts have warned.

Since early December [2007], Mozambique, Malawi, Zambia, and Zimbabwe have been hit by exceptionally heavy rainfall, which has caused floods described by meteorologists as the "worst in living memory".

Since early December [2007], Mozambique, Malawi, Zambia and Zimbabwe have been hit by exceptionally heavy rainfall, which has caused floods described by meteorologists as the "worst in living memory".

Already 45 lives have been lost in Mozambique, Zambia and Zimbabwe since the flooding began, while thousands of homes were washed away and vast swathes of crops were destroyed.

Zambian President Levy Mwanawasa last week [January 2008] declared the flooding a state of national disaster as heavy rains continued to fall in Zambia, Zimbabwe and Malawi, feeding into rivers running through Mozambique, particularly Zambezi.

The four countries lie on the Zambezi River Basin, an area that is prone to flooding owing to the presence of some of Africa's biggest man-made lakes. These are Cahora Bassa and Kariba, which has also recorded unusually high summer rainfall this season.

Power failures in Zimbabwe and Zambia due to collapsing electricity grids have become the immediate effects of the worsening floods but analysts feel famine would be the long-term consequence.

Thousands of Lives Are Disrupted

Zambezi River, the fourth largest in Africa, is already overflowing, threatening thousands of lives and crops downstream and heightening fears of a severe flooding season.

Last weekend, relief agencies estimated that close to 60,000 people have been displaced in Mozambique and a further 100,000 were at risk while in Zimbabwe around 2,000 were affected in the country's low-lying areas.

There are also reports of widespread destruction of large tracts of crop fields, with affected farmers already contemplating starting all over again.

Power failures in Zimbabwe and Zambia due to collapsing electricity grids have become the immediate effects of the worsening floods but analysts feel famine would be the long-term consequence.

Zimbabwe, which is in the middle of its worst economic crisis since independence 28 years ago [1980], is the hardest hit, with aid agencies already predicting a disastrous agricultural season.

The Zambezi River Basin

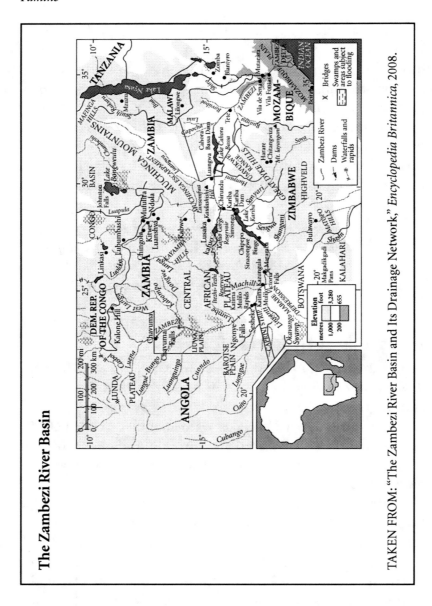

TAKEN FROM: "The Zambezi River Basin and Its Drainage Network," *Encyclopedia Britannica*, 2008.

According to the latest disaster alert issued by the Famine Early Warning System Network (FEWSNET), the floods have disrupted the entire agricultural season and destroyed productive assets such as cattle for most of Zimbabwe's rural peasants.

The former southern African economic powerhouse is struggling to feed itself and President Robert Mugabe's government had been pinning hopes of an economic turnaround on a successful agricultural season.

FEWSNET, which is an arm of the United States Agency for International Development (USAID), says effects of the 10-year-old economic recession would make it particularly difficult for Zimbabwe to recover from the floods, especially after successive years of droughts and failed cropping seasons.

"Zimbabwean government estimates indicate that, midway through December 2007, farmers had planted about 32 per cent more area under maize than had been planted around the same time last season," reads the report.

"However, in most parts of the country heavy rains since mid-December have slowed land preparation and planting and promoted weed growth. Most rivers are at risk of flooding and many low-lying areas have already been flooded."

Floods Have Destroyed Soil Nutrients

Excessive rainfall has also compromised the growth of established crops, particularly in low-lying fields where heavy clay soils have been water-logged. Fields with lighter, sandy soils have been leached of nutrients, added the report.

"Fertiliser is scarce this season, but even those farmers with access to fertiliser will not apply it if the rains continue with the same intensity," FEWSNET said.

Analysts say Zimbabwe's neighbours were better prepared to deal with the floods this time around because their infrastructure had improved.

In the 2000/2001 season when Southern Africa was hit by floods of a similar magnitude, Mozambique, which was still recovering from decades of civil war, was the worst affected, triggering a humanitarian crisis of huge proportions.

"Zimbabwe still had proper infrastructure and the authorities were able to contain the situation," said Mr Emmert Makombe, an agronomist based in Chiredzi, southern Zimbabwe.

"But this year without fertiliser and seed for replanting the situation is bound to be worse for our farmers."

No Chance for Recovery

This time there is no chance for recovery. One of the reasons Zimbabwe survived the Cyclone Eline-induced floods in the 2000/2001 farming season was because it still had a viable commercial farming sector and the economic problems blamed on Mr Mugabe's policies were just setting in.

But this time around the commercial farming sector is virtually non-existent after almost 4,000 white farmers were pushed off their land during a controversial land reform programme.

The chaotic land reform programme, which from inception has been condemned by international donors as unworkable and a recipe for disaster, is turning out to be just that.

In the more than six seasons the new black farmers have been on the land, the southern African country of about 12 million people has been facing a widening food crisis, as the land recipients struggle to gain experience.

The chaotic land reform programme, which from inception has been condemned by international donors as unworkable and a recipe for disaster, is turning out to be just that.

Production of cash crops such as tobacco and the staple maize continues to plummet, dragging the economy down with it. With the damage caused by the floods, the situation is bound to be worse, analysts warn.

The Need for Fertiliser

"A lot of fertiliser, especially ammonium nitrate or alternatively urea, will be needed to save crops in situations where the fields were not washed away," said Dr Alex Nyoni of the state-run Department of Agricultural, Technical and Extension Services (Agritex).

"But the fertiliser is not available and the little that is found on the black market is beyond the reach of the majority of farmers."

Zimbabwe requires 720,000 tonnes of compound D fertiliser and 774,000 tonnes of ammonium nitrate each year.

An increasing number of Zimbabweans can no longer feed themselves, with aid agencies saying more people in urban areas are in danger of starvation.

But this year all the manufactures say they can only produce 53,000 tonnes of compound D and 46,714 tonnes of ammonium nitrate subject to the availability of $12 million for spare parts and raw materials and an improvement in electricity supplies.

Agritex and its National Early Warning Unit (NEWU) and a team including the state-controlled grain monopoly, the Grain Marketing Board, the Meteorological Services Department, the Ministry of Agriculture, Central Statistical Office, farmers' unions, the Food and Agriculture Organisation (FAO) and FEWSNET are already planning a major crop assessment at the end of this month [January 2008] to determine the extent of the damage. FAO, in collaboration with its NGO [non-governmental organizations] partners, also plans a post-planting assessment next month.

Both assessments will focus on rural areas and are likely to provide more information on the impact of the floods on the season's crop production.

However, even before the assessments are carried out there are already fears of donor fatigue as food aid will not be restricted to the flood victims.

An increasing number of Zimbabweans can no longer feed themselves, with aid agencies saying more people in urban areas are in danger of starvation.

Failing Electricity Grids

Already, the floods have started wreaking havoc on Zimbabwe and Zambia's electricity grids, which have been disrupted by systems failure twice since the weekend. On Saturday, Zimbabwe and Zambia, as well as Botswana, were plunged into darkness after the inter-regional electricity grid collapsed.

In Zambia, the situation was normalised after eight hours while in Zimbabwe most parts of the country were still without power on Wednesday afternoon.

Electricity utilities in both countries said transmission pylons were collapsing under the weight of the heavy rains. Power and water failures have worsened in Zimbabwe dramatically in recent weeks and the Zimbabwe Electricity Supply Authority (Zesa) says it had no foreign currency to import spare parts to repair ageing equipment.

Famine in Malawi Is Worsened by HIV/AIDS

SouthScan

SouthScan *reports that the country of Malawi is the first country to experience a long-predicted new kind of famine brought about by a high rate of HIV/AIDS infection. The epidemic is so devastating in Malawi that farmers are unable to plant or harvest crops. The authors argue that because the government does not officially recognize the HIV/AIDS epidemic, many institutions such as the health care system and the military are in danger of collapse, further worsening the situation.* SouthScan *is an international publication providing political and economic analyses of the southern and central African region.*

As you read, consider the following questions:

1. What is the HIV infection rate in the Mulange district of Malawi?

2. To what does the health minister of Malawi attribute the high rate of mothers dying in childbirth, according to the authors?

3. According to the authors, what will unequal HIV/AIDS drug availability lead to?

SouthScan, "HIV Plus Famine Adds New Dimension to State Failure," *SouthScan*, vol. 20/21, October 21, 2005. Copyright Southscan Ltd. www.southscan.net. Reproduced by permission.

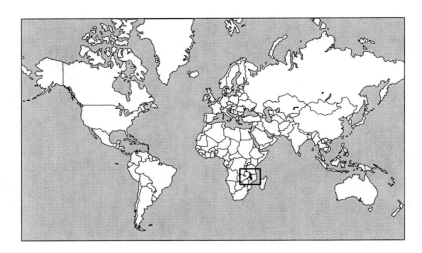

The food crisis in Malawi may become the first major example of the 'new variant famine' associated with the HIV/AIDS pandemic. Reports from the countryside indicate that the coping mechanisms of small farmers are collapsing under the weight of caring for the sick, or trying to bring in crops with fewer able-bodied family members.

Families in . . . [Malawi] are unable to cope when bread-winners are sick and unable to work or when households must shoulder the burden of caring for a mother or father with AIDS.

Up to five million people are in need of food aid in Malawi, the hardest hit in Southern Africa where five other countries are also struggling with extreme hunger that is expected to reach its peak in December [2005] and January [2006], according to the UN [United Nations] World Food Programme.

The southern Mulanje district bordering Mozambique is one of the worst-hit areas, and it also has an HIV infection rate at 29 percent, almost double the national average.

"You can't separate the two," John Makina, programme co-ordinator for the British-based charity organisation Oxfam in Mulanje, said. "We have had dry spells before but households used to be able to provide labour to get a bit of money and survive."

Makina says families in the Mulanje district are unable to cope when breadwinners are sick and unable to work or when households must shoulder the burden of caring for a mother or father with AIDS.

A New Kind of Famine

The concept of 'new variant famine' was popularised by researcher Alex de Waal, who has also sought to bring attention to the impending collapse of institutional structures because of the impact of the disease.

This has been an uphill struggle. He was also instrumental in initiating a UN response to the looming institutional crisis resulting from HIV/AIDS. The UN's Commission on HIV/AIDS and Governance in Africa (CHGA) will next month [November 2005] publish the results of research over two years into the likely effects of the pandemic on African states.

A special briefing was being held in Washington earlier this month at the Wilson Center with CHGA chairman KY Amoako, Pascoal Mocumbi, former prime minister of Mozambique and a CHGA patron, and Nana Poku, its director of research.

The maternal death rate in Malawi is now 1,800 per 100,000 live births, climbing from 620 two decades ago and 1,120 in 2000.

Meetings have been held in different African capitals over the past two years in an effort to elicit local information and to mobilise governments and organisations about the impact of HIV/AIDS down the line.

Famine and HIV/AIDS

The focus of Africa's latest food emergency is not only the arid, drought-prone Horn of Africa or Sahel regions, but also Southern Africa. Most of its countries are largely fertile, well watered and traditionally self-sufficient in food. One reason for Southern Africa's current crisis is that the region also has the world's highest HIV infection levels. The UN Joint Programme on HIV/AIDS (UNAIDS) estimated that infection rates in 2002 ranged from 15 per cent of adults in Malawi up to more than 30 per cent in Swaziland and Lesotho and a staggering 39 per cent in Botswana. Meanwhile, the World Food Programme (WFP) estimates that, as of March [2003], the number of people requiring food assistance in Zimbabwe stood at 7.2 million, or 52 per cent of the population. Nearly 8 million more also need food aid in Malawi, Zambia, Lesotho, Mozambique and Swaziland. . . .

The mechanics are chillingly simple. As farmers fall ill, physical weakness reduces their effectiveness and the area they cultivate shrinks, leading to declining crop yields. Food security is simultaneously jeopardized by the diversion of labour, time and money to deal with the illness. Agricultural households revert to subsistence rather than cash crop farming, bringing a fall in household incomes and the capacity to buy food. Family expenditures on health care rise, eventually consuming savings and other resources.

John Nyamu, "Famine and AIDS: a Lethal Mixture,"
Africa Recovery, vol. 17, no. 1, May 2003.

But many observers are still concerned at the continuing lack of official recognition for the impact of a pandemic that may cause the progressive failure of state structures. There remains sensitivity in government circles in South Africa and in the wider region to even using the term 'failed states', preferring the UN-inspired euphemism 'competent states' in the making.

Health System Collapse

Institutional failure is already being seen in Malawi, where the health sector is creaking as a result of loss of personnel, partly because of HIV and partly because of the brain drain to developed countries where pay and conditions are far superior to those in Malawi. Analysts see a vicious circle, with an increasing drain of skills until the economies and social conditions in their home states improve—unlikely to happen not least because of losses through HIV in the key sectors necessary for running the state.

Malawi has the third highest maternal mortality rate after Sierra Leone and Afghanistan, both emerging from protracted wars. The maternal death rate in Malawi is now 1,800 per 100,000 live births, climbing from 620 two decades ago and 1,120 in 2000. Women comprise 52 percent of the population, and 60 percent of the estimated 12 million population live below the poverty line of less than a dollar a day. The country has about 16,000 hospital beds.

The health minister attributed the high mortality rates to unsafe abortions, lack of emergency facilities and patients not receiving professional treatment due to a brain drain which has "reached a crisis point." Up to 120 registered nurses migrate to Britain and the United States every year.

Donors such as Britain, Norway and Sweden have launched a programme to reverse the flight of medical personnel by providing aid to double the salaries of medical workers to US$200 a month.

In Malawi life expectancy by 2000 had fallen to the country's 1969 level, essentially reversing 30 years of development investment.

Government Instability

The CHGA report is also likely to focus on the threat to state security because of personnel losses through the high rates of HIV in armies and police. These are generally reckoned to be above the national average by a significant factor. Governments are unwilling to admit to this because it is an acknowledgement of military weakness, say analysts, but in March 2003 Malawi's military commander, Gen. J G Chimbayo, said publicly that troop strength was down by more than 40 percent due to HIV deaths, with losses most acutely felt in the command-leadership structure. By 2004 troop strength had fallen to 50 percent of minimum capacity necessary to guarantee state security, according to a new report from the Washington-based Council on Foreign Relations.

Governments are overwhelmingly failing to respond to this element of the crisis. In South Africa the view in senior military and security circles is that treatment drugs will ensure that the command structure of the military remains intact while new and healthy recruits are brought into the ranks—though some military officials do not share this view and believe the middle level officers will be difficult to replace.

Governments may believe treatment drugs will also keep important echelons in other sectors, including in its own ranks and parliament, alive and working.

But in SA [South Africa] the roll-out of the free treatment drugs through state clinics programme is notably lagging and there is little sign of the nationwide mobilisation many believe is needed to cope with the disease.

Meanwhile analysts are warning that the inequity in making treatment drugs available to some and not all will eventually become transparent and will heighten social tensions.

But the SA government, the best endowed in the region, is not either preparing for the wider failure of states to its north—under the impact of AIDS or other factors—and is rather, in the view of analysts, responding on an ad hoc basis to the fallout. Thus SA, with its border controls progressively overwhelmed, has just agreed to the ending of visas for the floods of refugees from Zimbabwe while its officials make increasingly frequent calls for an end to rising xenophobia [fear of foreigners].

Tropical and Subtropical Countries Will Experience Famine Due to Climate Change

Sarah DeWeerdt

Sarah DeWeerdt, a Seattle-based science writer specializing in biology and the environment, argues that global climate change caused by humans burning fossil fuels will affect all aspects of people's lives. One of the most serious consequences of rising temperatures, she asserts, is dwindling crop yields, leading to malnutrition and famine. She states that although the poorer nations are least responsible for global warming, they will suffer the most. She points to the African nation of Mali to demonstrate that the projections are already coming true: temperatures are rising, and crop yields are dropping.

As you read, consider the following questions:

1. What did the local government of the Tigray region of northern Ethiopia do to increase the productivity of farmers' fields in the late 1980s?

2. What have farmers in Mali started to do to combat declining soil quality?

Sarah DeWeerdt, "Climate Change, Coming Home: Global Warming's Effects on Populations," *World Watch*, vol. 20, no. 3, May–June 2007, pp. 8–13. Copyright 2007 Worldwatch Institute, World Watch Magazine, worldwatch.org. Reproduced by permission.

3. According to environmental consultant Kristie Ebi, what is the problem with using fast growing crops to supply people with food?

Since the 1970s, rainfall has been scarce in the Sahel, the wide belt of semi-arid land that stretches across Africa on the southern edge of the Sahara Desert. One of the worst-affected areas has been the Tigray region of northern Ethiopia, where a series of prolonged droughts exacerbated by war caused widespread famine in the 1970s and 1980s.

To help increase the productivity of farmers' fields, the local government decided in the late 1980s to build a series of small dams to trap the unreliable rainfall and connect these to simple irrigation systems. Sure enough, harvests increased and fewer people went hungry—but health researchers also found that children in villages near the dams were seven times as likely to suffer from malaria. The water stored behind the dams provided perfect breeding habitat for the mosquitoes that carry the disease.

Most of the effects of climate change are likely to be harmful ones: declining agricultural production and more hungry people, increased spread of infectious diseases, dangerous heat waves and floods.

The people of this isolated rural region of Ethiopia offer a glimpse into the human future—a view of how global climate change can play havoc with populations' lives and livelihoods, and how addressing one climate-related problem can sometimes cause another. The World Health Organization (WHO) has calculated that by 2020 human-triggered climate change could kill 300,000 people worldwide every year. By 2000, in fact, climate change was already responsible for 150,000 excess deaths annually—deaths that wouldn't have occurred if we humans weren't burning vast quantities of fossil fuels and loading up the air with carbon dioxide and other greenhouse gases.

Jonathan Patz, a professor with the University of Wisconsin/Madison's Center for Sustainability and the Global Environment, praises the WHO's sober accounting as the most comprehensive, scientific estimate available of the health effects of climate change. The agency combined models of recent and projected climate change with data on several health dangers that are known to be affected by climate (including malaria, diarrheal diseases, and malnutrition) to calculate the disease burden due to changes in climate. However, Patz says, "their estimate is extremely conservative." Not only are the underlying assumptions conservative, but the analysis only concerns a few of the relatively better-understood health risks of climate change.

Climate change might have a few pluses for our species—for example, warmer winters probably mean fewer cold-related deaths in North America and Europe, while in some parts of the tropics hotter and drier conditions could reduce the survival of disease-carrying mosquitoes. But most of the effects of climate change are likely to be harmful ones: declining agricultural production and more hungry people, increased spread of infectious diseases, dangerous heat waves and floods. Although no region of the globe will be entirely spared, the negative effects are likely to fall most heavily on poor nations in tropical and subtropical regions. In other words, the people most vulnerable to the effects of climate change are precisely those who are least responsible for causing it—and those who have the least resources with which to adapt to it.

Climate Change Will Affect Crop Yields

"Malnutrition will very likely be one of the biggest impacts in low-income countries," says Kristie Ebi, an environmental consultant who has served on the Intergovernmental Panel on

Poor Nations Face the Greatest Risks

Two-thirds of the atmospheric buildup of carbon dioxide, a heat-trapping greenhouse gas that can persist in the air for centuries, has come in nearly equal proportions from the United States and Western European countries. Those and other wealthy nations are investing in windmill-powered plants that turn seawater to drinking water, in flood barriers and floatable homes, and in grains and soybeans genetically altered to flourish even in a drought.

In contrast, Africa accounts for less than 3 percent of the global emissions of carbon dioxide from fuel burning since 1900, yet its 840 million people face some of the biggest risks from drought and disrupted water supplies, according to new [2007] scientific assessments.

Andrew C. Revkin,
"Poor Nations to Bear Brunt as World Warms,"
New York Times, *April 1, 2007.*

Climate Change (IPCC) and several other climate change related scientific bodies. Globally, food production is likely to decrease only modestly at worst, but this overall pattern hides what many researchers see as a growing inequality between the haves and have-nots of the world.

Some relatively wealthy countries in temperate regions will likely see crop yields rise, mainly due to longer, warmer growing seasons. Even the excess carbon dioxide in the air that is the underlying cause of climate change can theoretically be a boon for agriculture, acting as a fertilizer when other conditions for plant growth are favorable. Though it's not yet clear whether or how this effect of carbon dioxide will play out in the real world, any beneficial effects are most likely to be seen at middle and high latitudes. The prospect of these changes causes skeptics of climate-change doom and gloom to envision vast stretches of northern tundra transformed into a future breadbasket.

One set of . . . calculations indicates that . . . continued "business as usual" greenhouse gas emissions would increase the ranks of the hungry by 80 million by 2080, mostly in Africa and southern Asia.

Meanwhile, however, crop yields are likely to fall in the tropical and subtropical world, latitudes with many poorer countries where most of the world's hungry and malnourished live today. There, many crops are already growing near the upper bound of their temperature tolerance, so further warming would push them beyond their limits. In some areas, precipitation may increase, causing crops to rot; elsewhere, rainfall may diminish and become more erratic, arriving unpredictably as intense downpours that will run off the parched earth instead of nourishing the soil. And since the economies of many poorer countries are heavily dependent on agriculture, the failure of crops at home will leave them unable to buy surplus grain abroad.

For the last decade and a half, Martin Parry of the U.K. Met (formerly Meteorological) Office (and current co-chair of the IPCC working group on impacts of climate change), Cynthia Rosenzweig of the Goddard Institute for Space Studies, and a large group of other researchers from various institutions have been modeling the possible effects of climate change on production of the world's staple grain crops: wheat, rice, maize, and soybeans. Their work integrates several complex computer models—of global climate, crop yields, world food trade, and various patterns of economic development and population growth—to predict future global agricultural production and the risk of hunger. One set of their calculations indicates that, accounting for future population growth, continued "business as usual" greenhouse gas emissions would increase the ranks of the hungry by 80 million by 2080, mostly in Africa and southern Asia.

If average temperatures in . . . Mali increase, as expected, another 2–3 [degrees centigrade] by the 2060s, potato yields could . . . decrease by about a quarter.

Already there are hints that such projections are beginning to come true. Recently, Ebi worked on a U.S. Agency for International Development study of possible adaptations to climate change in Zignasso, a town of about 3,000 people in the main agricultural area of southern Mali. "It's gotten hotter. It's gotten drier," she says of the area's climate. "Farmers are seeing the rains come at somewhat different times of year," and sometimes there are dry spells during the rainy season. To combat declining soil quality farmers have started adding more fertilizer to their fields of potatoes, the main cash crop, but nevertheless climate shifts mean that harvests are getting smaller.

If average temperatures in this area of Mali increase, as expected, another 2–3[degrees centigrade] by the 2060s, potato yields could further decrease by about a quarter. It's not clear whether rainfall in the area will increase or decrease. In general, scientists simply don't understand this part of the climate system very well, so different models often disagree in their predictions. But in either case, says Ebi, the soil will probably be drier, because warm temperatures cause soil moisture to evaporate more quickly—and that could spell trouble for rice, the area's staple grain crop.

As drier conditions shrink growing seasons in tropical and subtropical environments, farmers have been encouraged by governments and aid agencies to turn to new, fast-growing crop varieties: rice that matures in 90 days, for example, rather than 120 days. But this solution may beget its own set of problems, Ebi says: "The fast-growing cultivars, because they grow faster, have less time to absorb micronutrients" from the soil, so they might provide people with sufficient calories but leave them vulnerable to vitamin and mineral deficiencies. "We need to pay attention to the quality of the food, not just the quantity."

China and India Will Face Massive Food Shortages from Glacier Melt

Lester Brown

According to Lester Brown, the mountain glaciers of Asia are rapidly melting. Because agriculture in both Indian and China depend on water from rivers fed by annual ice melt, the eradication of the glaciers will lead to extreme food shortages in both nations. Further, China and India are taking too much water from underground resources, a practice that will also lead to widespread food shortages. Brown asserts that carbon emissions must be cut to avoid future famine, including banning new coal-fired power plants. Brown is the founder, president, and senior researcher at the Earth Policy Institute, an environmental research organization.

As you read, consider the following questions:

1. What percentage of the Ganges River's water flow comes from the Gangotri Glacier?
2. How many Chinese people died in the Great Famine of 1959–1961?
3. According to Brown, what led to the collapse of the Sumerian and Mayan civilizations?

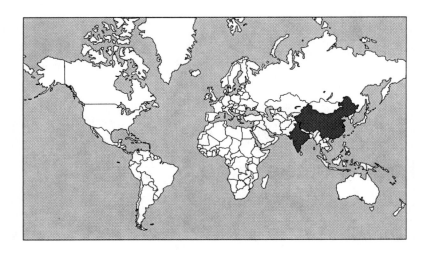

The world is now facing a climate-driven shrinkage of river-based irrigation water supplies. Mountain glaciers in the Himalayas and on the Tibet-Qinghai Plateau are melting and could soon deprive the major rivers of India and China of the ice melt needed to sustain them during the dry season. In the Ganges, the Yellow, and the Yangtze river basins, where irrigated agriculture depends heavily on rivers, this loss of dry-season flow will shrink harvests.

Melting Asian Glaciers Threaten the Food Supply

The world has never faced such a predictably massive threat to food production as that posed by the melting mountain glaciers of Asia. China and India are the world's leading producers of both wheat and rice—humanity's food staples. China's wheat harvest is nearly double that of the United States, which ranks third after India. With rice, these two countries are far and away the leading producers, together accounting for over half of the world harvest.

The Intergovernmental Panel on Climate Change [IPCC] reports that Himalayan glaciers are receding rapidly and that many could melt entirely by 2035. If the giant Gangotri Glacier that supplies 70 percent of the Ganges flow during the dry season disappears, the Ganges could become a seasonal river, flowing during the rainy season but not during the summer dry season when irrigation water needs are greatest.

Yao Tandong, a leading Chinese glaciologist, reports that the glaciers on the Tibet-Qinghai Plateau in western China are now melting at an accelerating rate. He believes that two thirds of these glaciers could be gone by 2060, greatly reducing the dry-season flow of the Yellow and Yangtze rivers. Like the Ganges, the Yellow River, which flows through the arid northern part of China, could become seasonal. If this melting of glaciers continues, Yao says, "[it] will eventually lead to an ecological catastrophe."

In India, where just over 40 percent of all children under five years of age are underweight and undernourished, hunger will intensify and child mortality will likely climb.

Overpumping Water Is a Cause for Alarm

Even as India and China face these future disruptions in river flows, overpumping is depleting the underground water resources that both countries also use for irrigation. For example, water tables are falling everywhere under the North China Plain, the country's principal grain-producing region. When an aquifer is depleted, the rate of pumping is necessarily reduced to the rate of recharge. In India, water tables are falling and wells are going dry in almost every state.

On top of this already grim shrinkage of underground water resources, losing the river water used for irrigation could lead to politically unmanageable food shortages. The Ganges River, for example, which is the largest source of surface water irrigation in India, is a leading source of water for the 407 million people living in the Gangetic basin.

In China, both the Yellow and Yangtze rivers depend heavily on ice melt for their dry-season flow. The Yellow River

Water for Crops in China and India: The Shrinking Glaciers of the Tibetan Plateau

Period	Number of Glaciers Studied	Percentage of Glaciers Retreating	Percentage of Glaciers Advancing	Percentage of Glaciers Remaining Stationary
1950–1970	116	53.44%	30.17%	16.37%
1970–1980	224	44.20%	26.30%	29.50%
1980–1990	612	90.00%	10.00%	0.00%
1990–2005	612	95.00%	5.00%	0.00%

TAKEN FROM: "An Overview of Glaciers, Glacier Retreat, and Subsequent Impacts in Nepal, India, and China," *World Wildlife Federation* Nepal Program, March 2005.

basin is home to 147 million people whose fate is closely tied to the river because of low rainfall in the basin. The Yangtze is China's leading source of surface irrigation water, helping to produce half or more of China's 130-million-ton rice harvest. It also meets many of the other water needs of the watershed's 368 million people.

The population in either the Yangtze or Gangetic river basin is larger than that of any country other than China or India. And the ongoing shrinkage of underground water supplies and the prospective shrinkage of river water supplies are occurring against a startling demographic backdrop: by 2050 India is projected to add 490 million people and China 80 million.

Social Unrest and Food Shortages

In a world where grain prices have recently climbed to record highs, with no relief in sight, any disruption of the wheat or rice harvests due to water shortages in these two leading grain producers will greatly affect not only people living there but consumers everywhere. In both of these countries, food prices will likely rise and grain consumption per person can be expected to fall. In India, where just over 40 percent of all children under five years of age are underweight and undernourished, hunger will intensify and child mortality will likely climb.

For China, a country already struggling to contain food price inflation, there may well be spreading social unrest as food supplies tighten. Food security in China is a highly sensitive issue. Anyone in China who is 50 years of age or older is a survivor of the Great Famine of 1959–61, when, according to official figures, 30 million Chinese starved to death. This is also why Beijing has worked so hard in recent decades to try and maintain grain self-sufficiency.

As food shortages unfold, China will try to hold down domestic food prices by using its massive dollar holdings to import grain, most of it from the United States, the world's leading grain exporter. Even now, China, which a decade or so ago was essentially self-sufficient in soybeans, is importing 70 percent of its supply, helping drive world soybean prices to an all-time high. As irrigation water supplies shrink, Chinese consumers will be competing with Americans for the U.S. grain harvest. India, too, may try to import large quantities of grain, although it may lack the economic resources to do so, especially if grain prices keep climbing. Many Indians will be forced to tighten their belts further, including those who have no notches left.

Ironically, the two countries that are planning to build most of the new coal-fired power plants, China and India, are precisely the ones whose food security is most massively threatened by the carbon emitted from burning coal.

Saving the Glaciers Means Saving Grain Harvests

The glaciologists have given us a clear sense of how fast glaciers are shrinking. The challenge now is to translate their findings into national energy policies designed to save the glaciers. At issue is not just the future of mountain glaciers, but the future of world grain harvests.

The alternative to this civilization-threatening scenario is to abandon business-as-usual energy policies and move to cut carbon emissions 80 percent—not by 2050 as many political leaders suggest, because that will be too late, but by 2020. . . . The first step is to ban new coal-fired power plants, a move that is fast gaining momentum in the United States.

Ironically, the two countries that are planning to build most of the new coal-fired power plants, China and India, are precisely the ones whose food security is most massively threatened by the carbon emitted from burning coal. It is now in their interest to try and save their mountain glaciers by shifting energy investment from coal-fired power plants into energy efficiency and into wind farms, solar thermal power plants, and geothermal power plants. China, for example, can double its current electrical generating capacity from wind alone.

Shrinking Harvests Lead to the Collapse of Civilizations

We know from studying earlier civilizations that declined and collapsed that it was often shrinking harvests that were responsible. For the Sumerians, it was rising salt concentrations in the soil that lowered wheat and barley yields and brought down this remarkable early civilization. For the Mayans, it was soil erosion following deforestation that undermined their agriculture and set the stage for their demise. For our twenty-first century civilization, it is rising atmospheric carbon dioxide concentrations and the associated rise in temperature that threatens future harvests.

At issue is whether we can mobilize to lower atmospheric carbon dioxide concentrations before higher temperatures melt the mountain glaciers that feed the major rivers of Asia and elsewhere, and before shrinking harvests lead to an unraveling of our civilization. The good news is that we have the energy efficiency and renewable energy technologies to dramatically reduce carbon dioxide concentrations if we choose to do so.

Periodical Bibliography

The following articles have been selected to supplement the diverse views presented in this chapter.

Africa News Service	"Climate Change a Deadly Threat to Africa," May 17, 2006.
Rob Crilly	"Africa Sinks Deeper into Despair as Famine Worsens; Continent Fails to Rebound from Drought, AIDS, Overpopulation," *USA Today*, May 22, 2006.
Anthony R. Daly	"The Famine Revisited," *Irish Literary Supplement*, vol. 27, no. 2, Spring 2008.
Alice Emasu	"Famine Imminent as Crops Rot," Africa News Service, September 22, 2007.
The Futurist	"Climate Change and Global Conflicts," March–April 2008.
Brian Halweil	"The Irony of Climate: Archaeologists Suspect That a Shift in the Planet's Climate Thousands of Years Ago Gave Birth to Agriculture. Now Climate Change Could Spell the End of Farming as We Know It," *World Watch*, March–April 2005.
Jakarta Post	"Famine, Drought, and Malnutrition: Defining and Fighting Hunger," July 3, 2006.
Roshni Menon	"Famine in Malawi: Causes and Consequences," *Human Development Report 2007–2008*, United Nations Development Programme, 2007.
Jason Motlagh	"Analysis: Hunger Grips the Horn," *UPI International Intelligence*, March 15, 2006.
Wairagala Wakabi	"Worst Drought in a Decade Leaves Kenya Crippled," *The Lancet*, vol. 367, no. 9514, March 18, 2006.

GLOBALVIEWPOINTS

CHAPTER 3

Famine, Politics, and the World Economy

Famine in Haiti Causes Political Unrest

Marc Lacey

Marc Lacey reports that hungry people in Haiti and around the world are rioting over food. Haitians stormed the presidential palace and caused the downfall of the prime minister. Likewise, according to Lacey, countries such as Egypt, Niger, and India are also experiencing social unrest due to food shortages. He contends that only outside investment will help Haiti, but that the political instability makes it unlikely that investors will want to take the risk. Lacey is a writer for the International Herald Tribune.

As you read, consider the following questions:

1. According to Lacey, what has set the world's poorer southern nations against the richer northern nations?
2. What was Haitian President René Préval's response to the people of his country who complained about rising food prices, according to Lacey?
3. What happened in 1974 during a famine in Niger?

Hunger bashed in the front gate of Haiti's presidential palace. Hunger poured onto the streets, burning tires and taking on soldiers and police. Hunger sent the country's prime minister packing.

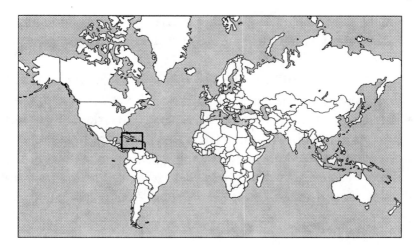

Haiti's hunger, that burn in the belly that so many here feel, has become fiercer than ever in recent days as global food prices spiral out of reach, spiking as much as 45 percent since the end of 2006 and turning Haitian staples such as beans, corn and rice into closely guarded treasures.

The food crisis not only is being felt among the poor, but also is eroding the gains of the working and middle classes, sowing volatile levels of discontent and putting new pressures on fragile governments.

Two Spoonfuls of Rice

Saint Louis Meriska's children ate two spoonfuls of rice apiece as their only meal two days ago and then went without any food the following day. His eyes downcast, his own stomach empty, the unemployed father said forlornly, "They look at me and say, 'Papa, I'm hungry,' and I have to look away. It's humiliating and it makes you angry."

That anger is palpable across the globe. The food crisis not only is being felt among the poor, but also is eroding the gains of the working and middle classes, sowing volatile levels of discontent and putting new pressures on fragile governments.

In Cairo, the military is being put to work baking bread as rising food prices threaten to become the spark that ignites wider anger at a repressive government. In Burkina Faso and other parts of sub-Saharan Africa, food riots are breaking out like never before. And in reasonably prosperous Malaysia, the ruling coalition was nearly ousted by disgruntled voters who cited food and fuel hikes as their primary concerns.

The Worst Crisis in Three Decades

"It's the worst crisis of its kind in more than 30 years," said Jeffrey Sachs, the economist and special adviser to the United Nations secretary general, Ban Ki Moon. "It's a big deal, and it's obviously threatening a lot of governments. There are a number of governments on the ropes and I think there's more political fallout to come."

Indeed, as it roils developing nations, the spike in commodity prices—the biggest since the administration of Richard Nixon—has pitted the globe's poorer south against the relatively wealthy north, adding to demands for reform of rich nations' farm and environmental policies.

But experts say there are few quick fixes to a crisis tied to so many factors, such as strong demand for food from emerging economies like China's; rising oil prices; and the diversion of food resources to make biofuels.

There are no scripts on how to handle the crisis, either. In Asia, governments are putting in place measures to limit hoarding of rice after some shoppers panicked at price rises and bought up everything they could.

Even in Thailand, which produces 10 million more tons of rice than it consumes and is the world's largest rice exporter, supermarkets have placed signs limiting the amount of rice shoppers are allowed to buy.

A Perfect Storm

"This is a perfect storm," President Elias Antonio Saca of El Salvador said Wednesday [April 16, 2008] at the World Economic Forum on Latin America in Cancún, Mexico. "How long can we withstand the situation? We have to feed our people and commodities are becoming scarce. This scandalous storm might become a hurricane that could upset not only our economies, but also the stability of our countries."

In Asia, if Prime Minister Abdullah Ahmad Badawi of Malaysia steps down, which is looking increasingly likely amid post-election turmoil within his party, he may be that region's first high-profile political victim of fuel and food price inflation.

In Indonesia, fearing protests, the government recently revised its 2008 budget, increasing the amount it will spend on food subsidies by 2.7 trillion rupiah, or about $280 million.

"The biggest concern is food riots," said H.S. Dillon, a former adviser to the Indonesian Ministry of Agriculture. Referring to small but widespread protests sparked by a rise in soybean prices in January [2008], he said, "It has happened in the past and can happen again."

Last month in Senegal, one of Africa's oldest and most stable democracies, police officers in riot gear beat and used tear gas against people protesting high food prices and later raided a television station that broadcast images of the event.

Many Senegalese have expressed anger at the government of President Abdoulaye Wade for spending lavishly on roads and five-star hotels for an Islamic summit that took place last month while many people are unable to afford rice, fish and cooking oil.

The Hungry Get Angry

"Why are these riots happening?" asked Arif Husain, senior food security analyst at the World Food Programme, which has issued urgent appeals for donations to help the Haitis of

---

A Hungry, Angry World: Locations of Food Protests and Riots, 2007–2008

Country	Date
Bangladesh	April 2008
Brazil	April 2008
Burkina Faso	February 2008
Cameroon	February 2008
Côte d'Ivoire	March 2008
Egypt	April 2008
Haiti	April 2008
India	November 2007
Indonesia	January 2008
Mozambique	February 2008
Senegal	March 2008
Somalia	May 2008
Yemen	April 2008

TAKEN FROM: Compiled by editor.

---

the world. "The human instinct is to survive and people are going to do no matter what to survive. And if you're hungry you get angry quicker. We see that around the world."

Leaders who ignore the rage do so at their own risk. President René Préval of Haiti appeared to taunt the populace as the chorus of complaints grew. He said if Haitians could afford cell phones, which many do carry, they should be able to feed their families. Then, later, he offered this zinger: "If there is a protest against the rising prices, come get me at the palace and I will demonstrate with you."

When they came, though, thousands of them full of rage and hunger, he huddled inside and his presidential guards, together with United Nations peacekeeping troops, rebuffed them.

Within days, opposition lawmakers had voted out Préval's prime minister, Jacques-Édouard Alexis, forcing him to reconstitute his government. Fragile in even the best of times, Haiti now walks on the edge, its population and politics both simmering.

"Why were we surprised?" asked Patrick Élie, a Haitian political activist who followed the food riots in Africa earlier in the year and feared they might come to Haiti. "When something is coming your way all the way from Burkina Faso you should see it coming. What we had was like a can of gasoline that the government left for someone to light a match to it."

Changing Menus

The rising prices are altering menus, and not for the better. In India, people are scrimping on milk for their children, and cutting back on luxuries like mutton for Sunday supper. Daily bowls of dal are getting thinner as each bag of lentils is stretched across a few more meals.

Maninder Chand, an auto-rickshaw driver in New Delhi, said his family had given up eating meat altogether for the last several weeks, forgoing the mutton curry they used to treat themselves to on Sundays.

Another rickshaw driver, Ravinder Kumar Gupta, said his wife had stopped seasoning their daily lentils with the usual onion and spices because the price of cooking oil was now out of reach. As vegetarians, the Guptas' chief source of protein is lentils, and these days, Gupta said, they simply eat bowls of watery, tasteless dal, seasoned only with salt.

On Hafziyah Street in central Cairo, peddlers selling food from behind wood carts bark out their prices. But few customers can afford to buy their fish or chicken, which baked in the hot sun, because of the inflation that has changed how they live and eat. Food prices have doubled in two months.

Ahmed Abul Gheit, 25, sat on a cheap, stained wooden chair by his own pile of rotting tomatoes. "We can't even find food in this . . . country anymore," he said, looking over at his friend Sobhy Abdullah, 50. Then raising his hands toward the sky, as if in prayer, he said, "May God take the guy I have in mind."

In Haiti, where three-quarters of the population earns less than $2 [U.S.] a day and one in five children is chronically malnourished, the one business booming amid all the gloom is the selling of patties made of mud, oil, and sugar.

Abdullah nodded, knowing full well that the "guy" was [Egyptian] President Hosni Mubarak.

The government's ability to address the crisis is limited, however. Egypt already spends more on subsidies, including gasoline and bread, than on education and health combined. As it struggles to keep up the subsidies, rising prices have eaten deeper into its budgets, and the pocket of average people.

"If all the people rise, then the government will resolve this," said Raisa Fikry, 50, whose husband receives a pension equal to about $83 a month, as she shopped for vegetables. "But everyone has to rise together. People get scared. But will all have to rise together."

That is the kind of talk that has promoted the government to treat its economic woes as a security threat, dispatching riot forces with a strict warning that anyone who takes to the streets will be dealt with harshly.

Remembering 1974 in Niger

Niger does not need to be reminded that hungry citizens overthrow governments. The country's first post-colonial president, Hamani Diori, was toppled amid allegations of rampant corruption in 1974 as millions starved during a devastating drought.

More recently, in 2005, it was mass protests in Niamey, the capital of Niger, that made the government sit up and take notice of that year's food crisis, which was caused by a complex mix of poor rains, locust infestation and market manipulation by traders.

"As a result of that experience the government created a cabinet level ministry to deal with the high cost of living," said Moustapha Kadi, an activist who helped organize marches in 2005. "So when prices went up this year the government acted quickly to remove tariffs on rice, which everyone eats. That quick action has kept people from taking to the streets."

Mud Cookies

In Haiti, where three-quarters of the population earns less than $2 [U.S.] a day and one in five children is chronically malnourished, the one business booming amid all the gloom is the selling of patties made of mud, oil and sugar, typically only consumed by the most destitute.

"It's salty and it has butter, and you don't know you're eating dirt," said Olwich Louis Jeune, 24, who has taken to eating them more often in recent months. "It makes your stomach quiet down."

But the quiet does not last long. And the grumbling in Haiti these days is no longer confined to the stomach. It is now spray painted on walls across the capital and shouted by demonstrators.

The outrage has been manipulated by Haiti's political spoilers, those who profit from the country's chaos. In recent days, Préval has patched together a response, using international aid money and price reductions by importers to cut the price of a sack of sugar by about 15 percent and trimming the salaries of some top officials. But those are considered temporary measures.

Solutions Will Take Years

The real solutions will take years. Haiti, its agriculture industry in shambles, needs to better feed itself. Haitians need jobs other than pushing wheelbarrows or scrounging scrap metal for pennies. Outside investment is the key, although that requires stability and not the sort of widespread looting and violence that the Haitian foot riots have fostered.

Most of the poorest of the poor suffer silently, too weak for activism or too busy raising the next generation of hungry. In the sprawling slum of Haiti's Cité Soleil, Placide Simone, 29, offered one of her five offspring to a stranger. "Take one," she said, cradling a listless baby and motioning toward four rail-thin toddlers, none of whom had eaten that day. "You pick. Just feed them."

Famine in Haiti Is Caused by International Banks

Brian Concannon Jr.

Brian Concannon Jr. recalls the Irish Potato Famine of 1845–1849, arguing that British economic policy was responsible for the over one million deaths that resulted from a potato blight in Ireland. He likens the Irish Famine to Haiti's situation in 2008. He asserts that the World Bank and the Inter-America Development Bank loaned money to Haitian dictators, and now are requiring steep payments. Concannon asserts that this policy is causing widespread hunger and starvation in Haiti and that the banks should cancel the debts. Concannon is a human rights lawyer and the director of the Institute for Justice & Democracy in Haiti.

As you read, consider the following questions:

1. Who was Sir Charles Edward Trevelyn?
2. Who were "Papa Doc" and "Baby Doc" Duvalier?
3. What did U.S. Representative Maxine Waters do in February 2008?

Saint Patrick is celebrated in Haiti, although not with the green beer and clothes he inspires in the United States. There he is better known as *Dambala*, a *loa* or spirit who of-

Brian Concannon Jr., "Saint Patrick Goes to Haiti," *Global Research*, May 1, 2008. www.globalresearch.ca. © Copyright Brian Concannon Jr., Global Research, 2008. Reproduced by permission.

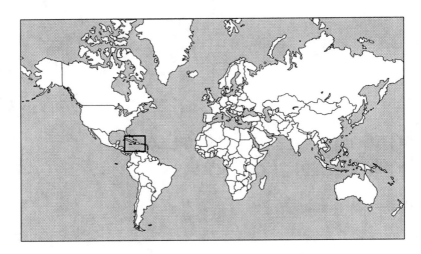

ten appears in the form of the snake in Haiti's Vodou religion. *Dambala* and the other spirits were brought from West Africa to Haiti in slave ships that brought the ancestors of today's Haitians across the Atlantic. Vodou was brutally suppressed, so the Haitians disguised their worship by representing their spirits with Christian symbols and icons. St. Patrick, often painted with snakes at his feet, and himself an escaped slave, must have seemed a good match. So centuries later, prints of St. Patrick with his staff and his bishop's mitre [hat], still preside over the drumming and chanting of vodou ceremonies in Haiti.

In the United States, St. Patrick is celebrated with sad songs that recognize the starvation and injustice that drove the ancestors of today's revelers across the Atlantic. One of the saddest and most popular of these songs, "The Fields of Athenry", can bring tears to your eyes, whether it is sung softly in the original folk version or shouted in the punk rock remake by the Dropkick Murphys. The song begins:

By a lonely prison wall
I heard a young girl calling
Michael, they have taken you away
For you stole Trevelyn's corn

So the young might see the morn
Now a prison ship lies waiting in
the bay.

At first blush this is personal tragedy—a young man deported from Ireland (to Australia), leaving his wife and young children behind, perhaps forever. All because he stole food to keep his kids alive. But with more context, the personal tragedy evolves into a natural and economic disaster, and eventually into an outrageous international injustice.

The Great Irish Famine

The song's Trevelyn is Sir Charles Edward Trevelyn, a British bureaucrat during the Great Irish Famine of 1845–1849. By 1845 Britain had controlled Ireland for centuries, during which the large British landowners (and a few wealthy Irish ones) had, with government help, pushed Irish peasants into smaller and smaller parcels. Although the Emerald Isle was a fertile country that grew more beef, grain and other food than it needed, most of that food was grown on large estates and exported to Britain. Irish peasants—the majority of the population—ate mostly potatoes because that was the only crop they could grow enough of to feed their families on their small plots. So when a fungus killed almost the entire potato crop in 1845 (and again for the next four years), the peasants had nothing to eat.

Sir Charles Trevelyn was responsible for managing the British government's relief efforts during the Famine. These efforts were the outrageous international injustice. British relief programs did save lives, but they did not come close to matching the need, because the government refused to take life-saving measures if they conflicted with its free-market economic theories. Trevelyn himself welcomed the famine as a "mechanism for reducing surplus population."

"Trevelyn's corn" was dried corn that the British government bought from the U.S. to distribute cheaply to the hungry. The government feared interfering with the free market more than it feared people starving to death, so it refused corn rations to anyone who could theoretically buy food on the market. This included people physically able to work but unable to find jobs in a collapsed economy, and families with any land—even a quarter acre. The economic theories did not fill empty stomachs, so people not theoretically poor enough for help starved to death while food sat undistributed in the warehouses.

Since 1980, when Haiti started receiving [help from the World Bank and the Inter-America Development Bank] in earnest, its per capita Gross Domestic Product (GPD) has shrunk by 38.3%.

Meanwhile, the potato blight did not affect other crops, including beef and grain. Ireland continued to be a net exporter of food throughout the famine. Keeping the food in Ireland would have saved lives, but it might have interfered with the free market. So the British kept eating beef and grain imported from a starving Ireland. Some Irish desperately ate their island's famously green grass: they were found dead, with green stains around their mouths.

Trevelyn's "mechanism" for reducing Ireland's population worked. Over one million people—by conservative estimates—were reduced to their graves, starved to death or killed by the diseases of hunger. More than 2 million were forced to flee the island—to America, England, Australia and many other places where St. Patrick is honored. All told, Ireland lost a quarter of its population.

Today, the Great Famine is as much a distant memory in Ireland as it is in Boston, New York or San Francisco. After centuries of being one of the poorest nations in Western Europe, Ireland is now one of the wealthiest and [most] peaceful countries in the world, the product of an economic boom fueled by strong government investment, especially in education and infrastructure.

Famine in Haiti: An Outrageous Injustice

But a century and a half after the Great Famine, people in Haiti are still being killed by the same economic theories. Haiti has made headlines recently, for people eating cookies made of salt, butter and brown dirt to hold off starvation. The stories were, at first blush, a personal tragedy (a mother unable to feed her infant son) and a natural and economic disaster (hurricanes, high fuel prices). But with more context, the personal tragedy evolves into an outrageous international injustice.

The Banks could simply cancel Haiti's debts, especially those from loans given to dictators, which would immediately make a million dollars a week available for life-saving government programs.

For decades, the World Bank and the Inter-America Development Bank (IDB) propped up Haitian dictators with generous loans. The notorious "Papa Doc" and "Baby Doc"—Francois and Jean-Claude Duvalier—received almost half of Haiti's current outstanding loans. The Duvaliers used the money to buy warm fur coats and fast cars, and to fund the brutal *Tonton Macoute* death squads. In return, the international community, especially the United States, received a reliable vote against [Cuban President] Fidel Castro in the United Nations and the Organization of American States.

The Haitian people received very little from these loans. Since 1980, when Haiti started receiving the Banks' help in earnest, its per capita Gross Domestic Product (GDP) has *shrunk* by 38.3%. Along the way, Haiti became the poorest country in the Americas, and one of the hungriest countries

143

Famines Caused or Worsened by Political Policy or Conflict

Dates	Region, Country, or Known As	Suggested Cause	Estimated Deaths
1845–1849	The Great Irish Potato Famine	British economic policy: potato blight	1.5 million (an additional 1.5 million left Ireland)
1931–1932	Ukrainian Holodomor (murder by famine)	Joseph Stalin, leader of the Soviet Union, intended to punish Ukrainian farmers who resisted collectivization	Over 7 million people died, most by starvation. At the height of the famine, 25,000 people per day were dying.
1941–1944	Siege of Leningrad	Siege of Leningrad, Soviet Union, by German forces during World War II	1 million people starved or froze to death
1943	The Bengal Famine	World War II; British colonial policy; governmental inaction	1.5 million to 3 million. (Some estimates range up to 5 million.)
1945	The Vietnamese Famine	The effects of World War II; Japanese occupation	1.5 to 3 million
1959–1961	The Great Chinese Famine	Natural disasters; Radical restructuring of China by Communist leadership	30 million or more
1984	Karamoja, Uganda	Drought, armed conflict, food insecurity	50,000; 25,000 of these were children; the loss represented 21% of the population
1996–1999	North Korea	Economic collapse and weather	600,000 to 3.5 million
1998–2008	Second Congo War	War	5.4 million died, mostly from starvation and diseases
2000–2008	Zimbabwe Food Crisis	Land reform policies: weather condition: AIDS	Ongoing crises; estimated that millions are at risk

TAKEN FROM: Complied by editor.

in the world. Today, [2008] about half of school-age kids in Haiti are not in school. Over half of all Haitians struggle to survive on $1 a day or less, and life expectancy is in the mid-50's. Many of those who can flee do so, [to] cities like Boston and New York, that sheltered the refugees from Ireland's famine.

The loans lavished on the Duvaliers and other dictators are now due, so Haiti's elected government is sending almost a million dollars every week to the well-appointed offices of the World Bank and the IDB in Washington. Like Ireland exporting beef while people starved, Haiti is exporting money while people die of poverty.

The World Bank and the IDB are not commercial banks. They are funded by our tax dollars, and were not established to make a profit. They are supposed to be, in the World Bank's words, "working for a world free of poverty." Like the British in Ireland, the Banks have their "relief programs" for Haiti, including programs that will eventually forgive a portion of Haiti's debt. But like the British response to Ireland's famine, the Bank programs do not rise to the seriousness of the situation.

Programs Are Too Little and Too Late

The Banks' programs are too late—they will not provide full relief for months, perhaps years. The Banks started their programs in 1996, but would not admit Haiti until 2007. Like the British declaring the starving Irish theoretically able to work, in 2000 the World Bank declared Haiti theoretically able to pay its debts, and therefore ineligible for the Bank's help: "[d]espite being very poor and having a relatively significant external debt level, . . . after taking advantage of other sources of debt relief, Haiti's debt . . . will be reduced to a sustainable level." So Haiti has just started jumping through the many hoops required to receive relief.

The Banks' programs are also too little—they stop where the requirements of helping poor people conflict with the requirements of the Banks' economic theories. The Banks could simply cancel Haiti's debts, especially those from loans given to dictators, which would immediately make a million dollars a week available for life-saving government programs. But the very institutions that gave generously to the Duvaliers—knowing full well how the money was being spent—now demand "accountability" from Haiti's democratic government before cancelling the dictators' debts. Accountability means, in part, that the government has an economic plan that satisfies the Banks' free market theories. Haiti's plan is not yet available, but the Banks have required other poor countries to demonstrate accountability by slashing public health and education spending. For now, accountability means keeping the $1 million coming every week, while the citizens of Haiti eat dirt.

This St. Patrick's Day [2008], as we sing about long-ago starvation and injustice [in Ireland], we should also think about the misery and injustice under St. Patrick's eyes in Haiti, an outrage we can still do something about.

The citizens of the United States could put a stop to this injustice immediately. We pay the largest share of the Banks' costs, and have the largest say in the Banks' governance. If our leaders made cancellation of Haiti's debt a priority, the debts would be cancelled.

Some members of the U.S. House of Representatives have taken the first step towards ending this injustice. In mid-February [2008] Rep. Maxine Waters circulated a letter that 53 of her colleagues signed, urging the U.S. Treasury Department to arrange the immediate suspension of all debts payments from Haiti. The Haiti Debt Cancellation resolution in the House, House Resolution 241, seeks to permanently cancel Haiti's IDB and World Bank debts, and has 66 co-sponsors.

In "The Fields of Athenry," Michael calls out his final words to his wife Mary:
Against the famine and the Crown
I rebelled, they cut me down
Now you must raise our child with
dignity.

If his children survived, Michael's wish would have eventually come true. Athenry, Ireland, is now a dignified tourist destination and commuter town, known for its quaint medieval buildings and ruins. People do not flee Athenry anymore, or steal corn to feed their children. Instead, people move there for jobs and opportunity—the latest census classifies one in five Athenry residents as "not Irish."

The children of "Michel" and "Marie" in Haiti deserve the same chance at dignity and prosperity that the children of Michael and Mary received. They can take a big step in the right direction if the international community lets Haiti's government invest in its people, their education and the infrastructure, rather than in payments to wealthy banks. So this St. Patrick's Day [2008], as we sing about long-ago starvation and injustice in what is now a wealthy island, we should also think about the misery and injustice under St. Patrick's eyes in Haiti, an outrage we can still do something about.

Indonesia's Government Must Protect Its Citizens from Famine

Jonatan Lassa

Conflicting definitions of the word "famine" stand in the way of appropriate responses to food crises in Indonesia, asserts Jonatan Lassa. Rather than argue over definitions, the government must institute a famine early warning system, urges Lassa. In addition, because there are increasing numbers of droughts caused by global climate change, the government must institute a drought management system that will provide food security and relief for the population. Lassa is the coordinator of the HIVOS program in Aceh, Indonesia. HIVOS is a Dutch relief non-governmental organization.

As you read, consider the following questions:

1. What do some local Indonesian non-governmental organizations see as the cause of food insecurity and famine in their country?
2. What percentage of babies born in Indonesia experience low birth weight due to malnutrition of the mothers?
3. According to Lassa, what does Food Security Regulation No. 68/2002 mention concerning the state's obligations to its people?

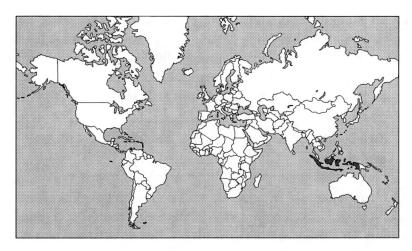

One of the hottest controversies in Indonesia today is the news about famine in Sikka district, East Nusa Tenggara, where about 60,000 people are at risk of starvation. One central government official, after visiting villages in the area, explained that there was no famine, arguing that the case was not a true famine such as in African countries. On the other hand, the district governments, religious leaders and NGOs [non-governmental organizations] claim that there is indeed a famine. While the media advocates through pictures, showing that a famine is occurring there.

A Double Shock

While from the local perspective, the community explained it very straightforwardly: they experienced the double shock of a sudden fall in the price of cacao, while at the same time pest attacks led to harvest failures. Consequently, the people experienced an income shock affecting their access to abundant food available at the local markets. The only buffer stocks, we are told by the media, are the famine foods locally known as Putak, made of palm leaves and wild tubers.

These conflicting views show huge gaps in understanding Indonesian modern "famine" and food insecurity determinants. Some local NGOs blame monoculture [one crop] agriculture as the underlying cause, as people (facilitated by the state a few years ago) experienced a livelihood change that led to the dependency on a commodity such as cacao that is prone to price fluctuations and pest attacks.

Famine should be seen as both a slow developing disaster and a process.

Famine should be seen as both a slow developing disaster and a process. Its occurrences differ very much from earthquakes and other natural disasters. The direct translation of famine to Bahasa Indonesian is *kelaparan*, which conveys an element of food shortages and severe hunger but not necessarily starvation.

How to Define Famine

[Famine researcher Dr. Stephen] Devereux argues about Western views of famine, which also have been adopted by the Indonesian government to some degree, I presume, as "a crisis of mass starvation" which entails three interacting conditions: food shortages, severe hunger and excess mortality. This definition was used by both central and provincial officials to argue that there is no famine in Sikka, and what is happening there is not the same as "African famine".

I would rather use [famine expert Dr. Jane] Walker's definition of famine as "a social-economic process which causes the accelerated destitution of the most vulnerable, marginal and least powerful groups in a community, to a point where they can no longer, as a group, maintain a sustainable livelihood. Ultimately, the process leads to the inability of individual to acquire sufficient food to sustain life". The bottom line here is that famine is a "process and not an event".

The challenge is how to capture local food systems with the existing tools of food insecurity monitoring and famine early warning. Many parties have developed food insecurity and famine indicators in Indonesia. To mention just two: the Agricultural Development Office (Bimas Pertanian) and the World Food Programme's Food Insecurity Atlas (FIA). The FIA, however, proved unable to provide an early warning for today's Sikka food insecurity.

The State Logistics Agency's food balance sheet cannot capture food insecurity at the micro-level. Two years ago, the Forum for Disaster Preparedness and Response (FKPB) developed a model called "Food and Livelihood Monitoring Systems". This conceptual model is very powerful as it helps portray the real conditions as it uses a livelihood approach to food insecurity and famine early warning. However, it does not work due to a lack of regular monitoring because of no funding support, apart from a lack of communications with stakeholders.

In 2003, 27.5 percent of children under the age of five in Indonesia were moderately to severely underweight.

Drought and Famine

Given that East Nusa Tenggara is one of the driest regions in Indonesia, it is obviously prone to drought. El-Nino southern oscillation-based droughts are increasing in terms of magnitude and frequency due to global climate change. The associated risks are lack of rainfall, water shortages, production failures, pests and disease, malaria, diarrhea and cholera, in which the combinations of such risks might lead to sporadic starvation and malnutrition.

However, drought is not the same as famine. Drought is a natural phenomenon which provides indications of potential threats to food security that may lead, though not necessarily, to famine. So far the government has used a hit-and-run approach to tackling the problem of chronic food insecurity.

States Must Feed Their Citizens

The State exists to feed people. Politicians proclaim defence or law and order or social issues or wealth creation or health as their priority. But without food, nothing else matters. For most of history, leaders were those who knew how to get it—sometimes by hunting prowess, sometimes by means of a gift for commanding herds, sometimes by naked power, forcing subjects to work in the fields and dig ditches, and sometimes by mediating with the gods or spirits of nature.

Food gave rulers their legitimacy. Rulers lasted only as long as they kept people fed. Today's leaders . . . have failed in this most elementary of obligations.

Felipe Fernandez-Armesto,
"Famine Could Eat Up the World—or Save It,"
The Times *(London, England), June 3, 2008.*

This is not a new criticism of the government, of course. However, I would recommend the government have a drought management strategy at the national level to be imposed in semi-arid and drought-prone areas.

At the macro-level, the implications of food insecurity make it clear that Indonesia is facing the risk of nutritional insecurity, where thousands of children might [be] trapped in severe malnutrition and experience a high mortality rate. An independent study showed that 14 percent of infants here experience low birth weights as a result of maternal malnutrition. On average, 16 percent of women aged 15–49 are suffering from a chronic energy deficiency. In 2003, 27.5 percent of children under the age of five in Indonesia were moderately to severely underweight.

The Government Must Protect Its People

One thing that I am sure of is that poor and marginal groups are the most prone to famine as they have the least human, social, financial and physical capital. The government should have an instrument of protection for citizens as part of its fundamental commitment to fulfill the International Covenant on Economic, Social and Cultural Rights, which was ratified by the Indonesian government after the 2004 tsunami.

Indeed, Food Security Regulation No. 68/2002 mentions the state's obligation to ensure food supplies and food stocks, to prevent and intervene in food insecurity (including food aid for the poor and price controls), and the roles of local governments and society in the elimination of famine and the assurance of food security.

Now is the time for the government to tackle both famine and food insecurity problems not according to the "old-fashioned model". Otherwise they should be called "famine lovers" for institutionally failing to develop a sustainable solution to food problems after 60 years of independence. The "famine lovers" might also include all the "relief-addicted" stakeholders, be it international NGOs, local NGOs or those in the UN who are pro-status quo.

Learning from the case of Sikka, be it a famine or a food crisis, the government should have a strong drought management strategy that is linked with food security monitoring, followed by annual contingency planning for relief intervention in drought-prone regions. Now is also the time for the government to enforce its own regulations on the protection of its citizens.

Worldwide Governmental Controls on Exports Will Cause Famine

Swaminathan S. Anklesaria Aiyar

Swaminathan S. Anklesaria Aiyar asserts that although rice and wheat prices are skyrocketing, world grain production remains high. He dismisses arguments that consumption is outstripping production or that the rush to ethanol is causing the price increases. Rather, he argues that export controls are artificially causing scarcity. Thus, rising prices are a predictable consequence of export controls. Aiyar believes that the only solution to the worldwide food shortages is for nations to work cooperatively and reduce export controls. Aiyar is a research fellow at the Center for Global Liberty and Prosperity at the Cato Institute, a nonprofit public policy research foundation.

As you read, consider the following questions:

1. How much of the United States corn crop has been diverted to ethanol?
2. What happens when all countries reduce their imports, according to Aiyar?
3. What was the original name of the World Trade Organization?

Swaminathan S. Anklesaria Aiyar, "Famine Mentality in a Time of Bumper Crops," *South China Morning Post*, May 15, 2008. www.cato.org. Copyright © 2008 South China Morning Post Publishers Ltd. All rights reserved. Reproduced by permission.

International rice and wheat prices have doubled or tripled in the last two years, but world grain production will reach a record high this year [2008]. So how come millions are falling into poverty and starting food riots across the world? The answer lies not in any outsized surge in world demand or fall in world supply, but in the fact that several countries, including China, have imposed duties, quotas and outright bans on agricultural exports. This has reduced the amount of grain available for world trade.

Record Harvests

The United Nations Food and Agriculture Organization [FAO] estimates that world production of cereals was a record 2,108 million tons in 2007, and will hit a new record of 2,164 million tons in 2008. Rice production will rise by 7.3 million tons and wheat by 41 million tons. World cereal consumption has been growing slightly faster (3%) than production (2%) for a decade, so global stocks have fallen to 405 million tons. But this is not a disaster scenario, and it hardly explains skyrocketing prices.

Countries imposing export controls, have, in effect, become hoarders themselves, creating an artificial scarcity in the world market, and an artificially high world price.

In the U.S., one-fifth of the corn crop has been diverted to ethanol, and in Europe, some vegetable oil has been diverted to biodiesel. These ill-conceived policies have induced farmers to switch significant acreage from wheat to corn, soybeans and rapeseed, but world wheat output has nevertheless risen from 596.5 million tons in 2006 to an estimated 647.3 million tons in 2008. Corn-based ethanol cannot explain the runaway increase in the price of rice, which grows in very different conditions.

155

Biofuels caused an initial spike in prices, which then led to panic, export protectionism and speculation in commodities futures—and these latter factors have increased prices much further. To protect domestic consumers from rising world prices, dozens of governments have curbed the export of rice and wheat—principally Argentina, Brazil, Russia, China, India, Ukraine, Vietnam, Cambodia, Pakistan, Egypt, and Indonesia.

The Consequences of Export Controls

Export controls have reduced the amount of rice and wheat available for world trade. The FAO estimates that world trade in rice will fall from 34.7 million tons in 2007 to 28.7 million tons in 2008, and trade in wheat from 113 million tons to 106 million tons. Actual trade may fall even more, as more and more countries impose export controls. Absent these limitations, it would be inconceivable for trade in grain to contract so sharply after record world harvests.

Countries limiting exports hope to reduce hoarding, which could send prices even higher. India has set limits on the stocks that each trader can hold.

But countries imposing export controls, have, in effect, become hoarders themselves, creating an artificial scarcity in the world market, and an artificially high world price. Farmers know what their crops could fetch on the world market, so they demand higher prices at home. And around and around we go.

This has eerie similarities to the Great Depression, when many countries resorted to import protection to protect jobs at home, and simultaneously devalued their currencies to try and push up exports. Yet the Great Depression got worse, thanks to what [economist] John Maynard Keynes called the fallacy of composition.

If one country alone resorts to import protection and devaluation, it can temporarily increase jobs. But at a global level, one country's exports are another's imports. If all coun-

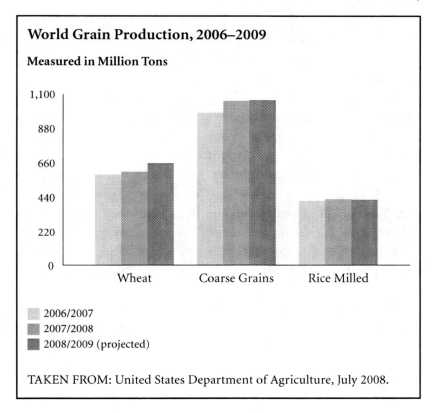

World Grain Production, 2006–2009

Measured in Million Tons

2006/2007
2007/2008
2008/2009 (projected)

TAKEN FROM: United States Department of Agriculture, July 2008.

tries reduce their imports, they unwittingly end up reducing their exports, too. And job losses get worse.

Today, each country wants to curb agricultural exports and stimulate imports to reduce prices. But if every country limits exports, the result is a decline in world imports, so prices rise instead of falling.

People are hungry, and it's not because there isn't enough food to go around.

The Need for International Action

Solving the problem may require coordinated international action. After the Great Depression, the world community created the Global Agreement on Tariffs and Trade—which later morphed into the World Trade Organization [WTO]—to negotiate simultaneous cuts in import barriers by major trading powers. This coordinated approach thwarted free riders, and gradually gained acceptance by all.

WTO rules permit food export limitations. In the Doha Round of trade negotiations, WTO has sought to reduce agricultural subsidies causing excess production. It never anticipated that export controls might create scarcities.

The new developments may improve the prospects of the Doha Round. But quick action is needed to tackle rising hunger. The WTO should convene an emergency meeting for countries to jointly reduce export controls. Even modest concessions can be in exporters' self-interest, as they would cause world prices to fall sharply, and thus ease domestic price pressures.

The terrible irony is that world grain production will be at a record high in 2008. People are hungry, and it's not because there isn't enough food to go around.

The Philippines Could Suffer Famine Caused by Political Corruption

Efren L. Danao

The Manila Times journalist Efren L. Danao reports that because government officials misused funds meant for the purchase of fertilizer, there may be a low-yielding rice harvest in the Philippines, leading to food shortages. In addition, corruption in government has led to smuggling, hoarding, and theft of rice supplies. Danao notes that the food authority has hired additional inspectors to try to stop the dishonest practices and make sure the emergency rice supplies reach the people who need them.

As you read, consider the following questions:

1. How much should rice from the Filipino food agency cost?

2. What are several ports used by smugglers of agricultural products, as mentioned by the author?

3. What are some of the problems with the food supply, according to the assistant manager of the National Food Authority?

Efren L. Danao, "Food 'Crisis' Preventable," *The Manila Times*, March 18, 2008. Copyright 2008 McClatchy-Tribune Information Services. Reproduced by permission.

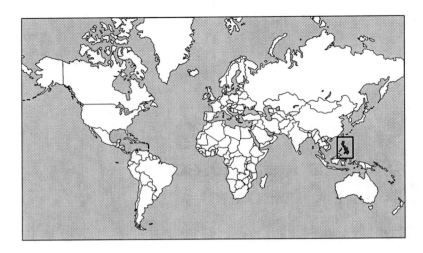

Senate President Manuel Villar Jr. blamed Malacañang [the official residence of the President of the Philippines] for a supposedly looming food crisis, which, he said, could have been averted had the government used a P [Peso; Philippine currency] 720 million fertilizer fund properly in 2004.

Villar on Monday [March 2008] told a press conference that they could now see in the reported rice shortage in parts of the country the ill effects of Malacañang's lack of cooperation with the Senate in the investigation of an alleged scam that caused dissipation of the P720-million fund.

The amount, supposedly for the purchase of fertilizers, was used instead to buy overpriced and virtually useless chemicals as shown in a Senate inquiry.

[Filippino Senator Manuel Roxas] predicted that the rice crisis will worsen after October [2008] since there is a two-month deficit supply of rice for consumption.

Former Agriculture Undersecretary Jocelyn "Joc-Joc" Bolante, the project head, has been hiding and has avoided clarifying his role in the fertilizer scam.

"If there is low rice production now, one of the reasons are the missing fertilizers," Villar said.

Rice Traders Are Making the Crisis Worse

Sen. Manuel "Mar" Roxas 2nd said rice traders are deepening the supposed rice crisis by rebagging the cheap rice from the National Food Authority (NFA) and selling it as commercial rice. Rice from the agency should cost only P18 a kilo but Roxas said no rice is now available at that price.

"The NFA is supposed to help impoverished citizens but the black markets get a big run of their money," Roxas added.

He predicted that the rice crisis will worsen after October [2008] since there is a two-month deficit supply of rice for consumption.

"Where will we get our supply from?" Roxas asked. "We cannot depend anymore on other country's exports. India will be consuming for itself."

He lashed out at the proposal to solve the crisis by limiting the people's food intake.

"Whoever suggested that must have been well-off because the only problem rich people have is they are fat. But for the poor who only eat rice, soy sauce and salt, that's all they [will] ever have. How much more if they have to limit their rice intake?" Roxas asked.

A Proposal to the Philippines Government

He proposed that the national government release the calamity fund for local governments so they can make sure that they will not run out of supplies. He also called for new, more effective programs for agriculture, build more irrigation systems and farm-to-market roads, and stop converting farms into residential and commercial lots.

Food shortage in the country has assured by the unabated influx of imported agricultural products, according to AGAP [a Filipino political party] party-list Rep. Nicanor Briones.

161

A Favorite Scam in the Philippines

Searches by agencies such as the National Bureau of Investigation, the National Food Authority and the Presidential Anti-Smuggling Group appear, however, to have barely scratched the surface of what is a perennial problem here. . . .

One favorite scam of rice traders is to repackage 50-kilogram bags that the government distributes to poor areas at nearly half the current price of 32 pesos, or US$0.80, per kilogram. Investigators discovered just one warehouse implicated in the racket—next to none compared with the scores of warehouses believed to be involved in such rackets routinely.

Donald Kirk,
"Anti-Chinese Cracks in Philippine Rice Bowls,"
Asia TimesOnline, April 3, 2008. www.atimes.com.

As a result, he said, the Philippines will have to rely on imported goods in 10 to 20 years. By the time, he added, producers will have abandoned rice farming and raising livestock.

Corruption in Customs

The allegedly rampant smuggling, Briones said, is tolerated by inept and corrupt officials of the Bureau of Customs also allegedly in connivance with smugglers bringing in agricultural products untaxed.

He has filed House Bill 3110 and Quezon Rep. Lorenzo Tanada 3rd House Bill 15 to curb the unchecked smuggling.

Briones said many backyard hog and poultry raisers who contribute as much as 70 percent of the swine and chicken supplies to the market have shifted to other businesses.

He added that companies engaged in hog and chicken production are cutting down on their production.

Briones had sought investigation of the alleged smuggling of agricultural products through House Resolution 308.

Smuggling Is Rampant

Information gathered by his group, Briones said, showed that the smuggling of agricultural products is unabated in free ports, such as Clark and Subic, and in major Philippine ports, such as the North Harbor and South Harbor in Manila, and in Cebu and Batangas.

In the Bicol Region, the provincial government of Albay is apparently bracing for the food crisis. It is set to release this week a P21.5-million rice loan to 15 towns and three cities as seed capital of local governments to operate National Food Authority outlets in Legazpi City.

Among the "dirty tricks" used by crooked merchants are hoarding, mixing government rice with commercial rice, passing off government rice as commercial rice, and filling empty sacks of commercial brands with government rice.

Gov. Joey Salceda of Albay told *The Manila Times* that this fund will be used by the local units to subsidize rice from the food authority to ensure cheap rice and access to it by poor families. He said the P21.5-million credit line at zero interest is payable in six months.

Salceda said the rice shortage in the province had been caused by floods, landslides and lack of supply. He added that climate change had also adversely affected agricultural production in the region, especially that of rice.

Rice shortages have also been reported in neighboring Camarines Sur and Sorsogon provinces.

Rice from Vietnam

At this writing, at least 260 bags of rice from Vietnam that will augment stock of the National Food Authority were being unloaded at the Tabaco City International Seaport.

In Cavite province near Manila, the food authority has stepped up its drive against merchants using various tricks to sell otherwise cheaper government-subsidized rice at much higher prices.

Jaime Hadlocon, the agency's assistant manager there, told *The Times* that he has deputized additional inspectors, leading to the recent arrest of some retailers in Dasmarinas and Silang towns and Cavite City for selling government rice at P27 to P29 per kilo instead of its subsidized price of P18.25 a kilo. These traders face fines of at least P2,000, suspension for months of their permit to sell rice, or perpetual disqualification from getting allocations from the food authority.

Hadlocon said that among the "dirty tricks" used by crooked merchants are hoarding, mixing government rice with commercial rice, passing off government rice as commercial rice, and filling empty sacks of commercial brands with government rice.

Food experts also feared that by 2010, one kilo of rice might cost more than one liter of oil.

Despite such tricks, he added, there will be no rice shortage in Cavite because he makes sure that there are 30,000 bags of rice (good for 45 days) in their provincial warehouse.

Hadlocon said the food supply is beset with serious problems, such as unpredictable changes in climate causing damages to crops, high price of imports, protective trade policies of supplying countries, rising prices of fertilizers, insufficient irrigation, few farm-to-market roads, conversion of agricultural areas to housing subdivisions, and raising crops for use not as food but as sources of alternative fuel.

He cited the agency's studies showing that daily wastage in rice amounts to 25,000 sacks, or P22-million worth of rice, and that it takes 5,000 liters of water to produce just one kilo of rice. Hadlocon said food experts also feared that by 2010, one kilo of rice might cost more than one liter of oil.

Biofuels Cause Worldwide Famine

George Monbiot

British political analyst George Monbiot argues that using food crops to produce biofuels will cause further food shortages. In addition, he asserts, the total impact of using biofuels, including the cost and production of nitrogen fertilizers, will create more global warming than petroleum fuels. He maintains that rather than providing a new source of income for small farmers, biofuels will encourage corporations and governments to clear the land of small farmers to make room for large plantations of sustainable biofuel crops. He believes this is a crime against humanity.

As you read, consider the following questions:

1. What was the percentage of increase in the cost of rice between 2006 and 2007, according to Monbiot?
2. What greenhouse gas does nitrogen fertilizer release, according to Monbiot?
3. What is jatropha?

It doesn't get madder than this. Swaziland is in the grip of a famine and receiving emergency food aid. Forty per cent of its people are facing acute food shortages. So what has the government decided to export? Biofuel made from one of its staple crops, cassava. The government has allocated several thousand hectares of farmland to ethanol production in the district of Lavumisa, which happens to be the place worst hit by drought. It would surely be quicker and more humane to refine the Swazi people and put them in our tanks. Doubtless a team of development consultants is already doing the sums. This is one of many examples of a trade that was described last month [October 2007] by Jean Ziegler, the UN's special rapporteur, [on the right to food; 2000–2008] as "a crime against humanity". Ziegler took up the call . . . for a five-year moratorium on all government targets and incentives for biofuel: the trade should be frozen until second-generation fuels—made from wood or straw or waste—become commercially available. Otherwise, the superior purchasing power of drivers in the rich world means that they will snatch food from people's mouths. Run your car on virgin biofuel, and other people will starve.

Biofuels Will Raise Food Prices

Even the International Monetary Fund, always ready to immolate the poor on the altar of business, now warns that using food to produce biofuels "might further strain already tight supplies of arable land and water all over the world, thereby pushing food prices up even further". This week [November 2007], the UN Food and Agriculture Organisation will announce the lowest global food reserves in 25 years, threatening what it calls "a very serious crisis". Even when the price of food was low, 850 million people went hungry because they could not afford to buy it. With every increment in the price of flour or grain, several million more are pushed below the breadline.

The cost of rice has risen by 20% over the past year, [since 2006] maize by 50%, wheat by 100%. Biofuels aren't entirely to blame—by taking land out of food production they exacerbate the effects of bad harvests and rising demand—but almost all the major agencies are now warning against expansion. And almost all the major governments are ignoring them.

Avoiding Hard Political Choices

They turn away because biofuels offer a means of avoiding hard political choices. They create the impression that governments can cut carbon emissions and—as Ruth Kelly, the British transport secretary, announced last week—keep expanding the transport networks. New figures show that British drivers puttered past the 500 [billion] kilometre mark for the first time last year [2006]. But it doesn't matter: we just have to change the fuel we use. No one has to be confronted. The demands of the motoring lobby and the business groups clamouring for new infrastructure can be met. The people being pushed off their land remain unheard.

[Research] suggests that protecting uncultivated land saves, over 30 years, between two and nine times the carbon emissions you might avoid by ploughing it and planting biofuels.

In principle, burning biofuels merely releases the carbon the crops accumulated when growing. Even when you take into account the energy costs of harvesting, refining and transporting the fuel, they produce less net carbon than petroleum products. The law the British government passed a fortnight ago [October 2003]—by 2010, 5% of our road transport fuel must come from crops—will, it claims, save between 700,000 and 800,000 tonnes of carbon a year. It derives this figure by framing the question carefully. If you count only the immediate carbon costs of planting and processing biofuels, they appear to reduce greenhouse gases. When you look at the total impacts, you find they cause more warming than petroleum.

The Costs of Biofuels

Biofuels aren't really necessarily a source of energy, in the sense of producing more energy than they consume in production, another is that they have the potential for exacerbating hunger worldwide. On the first point; Cornell researcher David Pimentel has tracked the energy costs of producing ethanol and biodiesel from various agricultural sources, including the energy needed to plant, grow and harvest the corn, the fertilizer and pesticides used on it, the energy costs of transporting, the plant matter and the energy used in production, and found that in virtually every case, there is more energy input than taken out of it. Others have found slight net positives energy accruals. . . . If something is dependent for 95% of its energy value on the availability of fossil fuels, we can expect both its price and availability to be constrained by fossil fuel costs and constraints.

The impact of biofuels on world hunger can be reduced to simple land use mathematics. For example, were we to convert all 179,000,000 hectares of arable land in the US to biofuel production, we might be able to meet much of our present energy needs. We would, however, grow no food, and we would strip our soil even more severely than we have thus far. . . . Meat eating and biofuel production are already raising the price of grain, a cost that adversely affects the poorest people in the world. They already spend 50% or more of their income on food, so the 25% rise in grain prices we are already experiencing means less food in people's bellies.

Sharon Astyk, "Ethics of Biofuels,"
Energy Bulletin, *December 28, 2006.*
www.energybulletin.net.

Nitrogen Fertilizers and Greenhouse Gases

A recent study by the Nobel laureate Paul Crutzen shows that the official estimates have ignored the contribution of nitrogen fertilisers. They generate a greenhouse gas—nitrous oxide—that is 296 times as powerful as CO_2 [carbon dioxide]. These emissions alone ensure that ethanol from maize [corn] causes between 0.9 and 1.5 times as much warming as petrol, while rapeseed [canola] oil (the source of more than 80% of the world's biodiesel) generates 1–1.7 times the impact of diesel. This is before you account for the changes in land use.

A paper published in the journal *Science* three months ago [August 2007] suggests that protecting uncultivated land saves, over 30 years, between two and nine times the carbon emissions you might avoid by ploughing it and planting biofuels. Last year the research group LMC International estimated that if the British and European target of a 5% contribution from biofuels were to be adopted by the rest of the world, the global acreage of cultivated land would expand by 15%. That means the end of most tropical forests. It might also cause runaway climate change.

The British government says it will strive to ensure that "only the most sustainable biofuels" will be used in the UK. It has no means of enforcing this aim—it admits that if it tried to impose a binding standard it would break world trade rules. But even if "sustainability" could be enforced, what exactly does it mean? You could, for example, ban palm oil from new plantations. This is the most destructive kind of biofuel, driving deforestation in Malaysia and Indonesia. But the ban would change nothing. As Carl Bek-Nielsen, vice chairman of Malaysia's United Plantations Berhad, remarked: "Even if it is another oil that goes into biodiesel, that other oil then needs to be replaced. Either way, there's going to be a vacuum and palm oil can fill that vacuum." The knock-on effects cause the destruction you are trying to avoid. The only sustainable bio-fuel is recycled waste oil, but the available volumes are tiny.

If there is one blindingly obvious fact about biofuel, it's that it is not a smallholder crop.

At this point, the biofuels industry starts shouting "jatro-pha". It is not yet a swear word, but it soon will be. Jatropha is a tough weed with oily seeds that grows in the tropics. This summer [Irish rock star] Bob Geldof, who never misses an opportunity to promote simplistic solutions to complex prob-lems, arrived in Swaziland in the role of "special adviser" to a biofuels firm. Because it can grow on marginal land, jatropha, he claimed, is a "life-changing" plant that will offer jobs, cash crops and economic power to African smallholders.

Yes, it can grow on poor land and be cultivated by small-holders. But it can also grow on fertile land and be cultivated by largeholders. If there is one blindingly obvious fact about biofuel, it's that it is not a smallholder crop. It is an interna-tionally traded commodity that travels well and can be stored indefinitely, with no premium for local or organic produce. Already the Indian government is planning 14m hectares of jatropha plantations. In August [2007], the first riots took place among the peasant farmers being driven off the land to make way for them.

If the governments promoting biofuels do not reverse their policies, the humanitarian impact will be greater than that of the Iraq war. Millions will be displaced, hundreds of millions more could go hungry. This crime against humanity is a complex one, but that neither lessens nor excuses it. If people starve because of biofuels, Ruth Kelly and her peers will have killed them. Like all such crimes, it is perpetrated by cowards, attacking the weak to avoid confronting the strong.

Periodical Bibliography

The following articles have been selected to supplement the diverse views presented in this chapter.

Sharon Astyk	"Ethics of Biofuels," *Energy Bulletin*, December 28, 2006.
Alan Beattie	"Governments Can No Longer Ignore the Cries of the Hungry," *The Financial Times*, April 5, 2008.
Prabha Jagannathan	"Safety Net: Price Control on Food Might Not Help the Needy," *The Economic Times*, April 18, 2008.
Simon Jenkins	"Comment & Debate: The Cost of Green Tinkering Is in Famine and Starvation," *The Guardian*, April 16, 2008.
New York Times	"Politics and Hunger," June 9, 2008.
Pilirani Semu-Banda	"Malawi: Resentment Lingers After Famine Triggered by IMF," Inter Press Service News Agency, March 20, 2007.
Kay Seok	"North Korea Is Headed Toward Anther Famine: An Aid Gap," *International Herald Tribune*, May 4, 2006.
Lewis Smith and Francis Elliott	"Rush for Biofuels Threatens Starvation on a Global Scale: Food Shortages," *The Times* (London, England), March 7, 2008.
K. Subramanian	"The Fund, Fed, and Finance Feed the Famine," *The Hindu Business Line*, May 16, 2008.
Paranjoy Guha Thakura	"India: Blames West for High Food, Energy Prices," *Terraviva Europe*, April 30, 2008.
John Vidal	"Global Rush to Energy Crops Threatens to Bring Food Shortages and Increase Poverty, Says UN," *The Guardian*, May 9, 2007.

GLOBALVIEWPOINTS

CHAPTER 4

Responses to Famine

Responding to Global Famine: An Overview

Tara K. Dix

Former associate editor of U.S. Catholic *magazine Tara K. Dix argues that although addressing famine is a mighty task, there are effective responses to the problem of world hunger. She cites several organizations that are successfully providing help, including Heifer International, Bread for the World, and Opportunity International. In addition, she asserts that biotechnology will improve crop productivity. Finally, she argues that supporting local farmers helps sustain food production. She offers five practical suggestions for how people can join the fight against global hunger.*

As you read, consider the following questions:

1. What is the secret of Heifer International's success, according to Ray White, one of Heifer's directors?

2. What five elements must be implemented at the same time to successfully address the problem of hunger, according to Jeffrey Sachs, founder of Millennium Promise?

3. What is Opportunity International, and what does it do to help those in need?

Tara K. Dix, "Recipe for a Hungry Planet: Feeling Helpless About Starving Children in Asia or Even Next Door?" *U.S. Catholic*, October 2007, pp. 12–17. Copyright © 2007 by Claretian Publications. Reproduced by permission.

Facts are facts: There is enough food in the world to feed the world. So why do 1 billion still go hungry? Why do 30,000 [die] every day of starvation? And why does the number of hungry people rise at a rate of 5 million per year?

Catholic Relief Services' food aid expert William Lynch says it is quite simply a lack of desire. "Of course there is enough food to give to those who need it," he says. "But is there the will? Absolutely not."

A Herculean Task

Most agree the eradication of hunger and poverty depends on a combination of person-to-person compassion in the form of organized aid as well as an overhaul of societal and civic structures that prevent equitable access to food. The task seems Herculean, and the average Joe is easily discouraged.

Still, one would be hard-pressed to find a person of faith who doesn't see feeding the hungry as part of a Christian's duty. "The theme of meals and eating permeates the gospels," says Mark Brinkmoeller, director of church relations for Bread for the World, an anti-hunger organization. "In the Gospel of Matthew, Jesus says, 'Whom have you fed?' And we will be judged on this. This is intrinsic to our faith."

About 8 percent of child deaths from starvation are a result of emergency food shortage.

Sen. George McGovern, former ambassador to the United Nations' food agency and coauthor of *Ending Hunger Now*, puts it in blunt terms: "If we fail to do this, we will stand condemned before the bar of history. In that case, shame on you, and shame on me."

The Trap of Poverty

The biggest problem facing the hungry is the poverty trap: the cyclical combination of no money, no food, and no health care. Malnutrition leads to illness; illness drains financial resources; drained finances lead to malnutrition. Factor in a lack of access to education, financial services, or credit—all of which prevent upward economic mobility—and you've got a person who is—in a word—trapped.

On the international scene, we see photographs of emaciated victims of famine caused by drought, civil war, or natural disaster. We see children with distended bellies and vacant eyes, collarbones and shoulder blades protruding. These are the extreme, but all too frequent, cases. About 8 percent of child deaths from starvation are a result of emergency food shortage.

When the tsunami hit Asia at 9:26 a.m. on Dec. 26, 2004, Catholic Relief Services and its partners were serving emergency meals by lunchtime.

In our own country we may not see hunger the way we can in the midst of international crises, but it's there: in students who can't concentrate because their stomachs are empty, in elderly people who skip meals, and in parents who forego their own needs so that their kids can eat. America's Second Harvest [food bank] served 25.3 million Americans with emergency food aid last year [2006], including almost 9 million children.

Meanwhile thousands of people look for ways to fill all these empty bellies, and among them a thousand different approaches can be found. Here are five of those ways and what you can do to join the effort.

Give People Animals

The most obvious way to help hungry people is, of course, to give them food. Countless groups here and abroad raise money for direct food aid, distributing meals to people in crisis.

When the tsunami hit Asia at 9:26 a.m. on Dec. 26, 2004, Catholic Relief Services [CRS] and its partners were serving emergency meals by lunchtime. For months they continued to provide food and shelter for the displaced victims until they could get back on their feet.

Direct food aid serves an immediate need—an emergency situation. CRS, and many others like it, also seeks to establish programs that will serve the long-term needs of the community: sufficient nutrition, health care, education, and employment.

Out of the 3 billion poorest people in the world, only 10 million have insurance.

The secret to Heifer International's success is that animals reproduce, says Ray White, one of Heifer's directors, of the worldwide organization that provides domestic animals to needy families in the United States and abroad. "If you put two tractors together, you don't get a third tractor," he says.

From water buffalo, cows, and sheep to rabbits, chickens, and honeybees, Heifer provides animals that will be a source of income, food, or both, and gives people the tools they will need to succeed, like training in animal care, agricultural techniques, finances, marketing, reading, and writing. Recipients promise to pass on the gift by donating at least one of their animal's offspring to a neighbor in need.

"It's amazing how one small animal can completely change the life of a family," White says.

White recently returned from a Heifer project in Nepal, where a women's cooperative received a small herd of goats several years ago. The co-op now has more than $10,000 in a bank savings account and was able to pass on 56 goats—more than they started with—to another women's co-op.

Hunger Is a Political Problem

CRS' Lynch recently returned from Haiti, where the average person is experiencing a 460-calorie food deficit per day. "That's lunch. Everybody there is missing a meal every single day."

Lynch points to a change in government policies to gain ground in the battle against hunger. "Ending hunger is possible," he says, "but we have to overcome something in our nature. As Catholics, we don't demand of our Catholic legislators that they support a preferential option for poor, but we do judge them on certain other policy points."

With the 2008 presidential campaign already underway, it will be up to concerned Americans to make sure poverty relief has a place on each candidate's agenda. Lynch sizes up the problem: "There's no constituency for the poor. Their vote is not a significant voice." So who will speak for them?

In the United States it takes an average of 16 pounds of grain fed to cows to produce one pound of beef.

Bread for the World (BFW) believes that hunger is indeed a political problem, so it lobbies the U.S. government to adopt or strengthen legislation that will get food to those who need it. BFW looks both at domestic hunger—including dispelling the myth that there is no domestic hunger with facts such as "14 million children live in households where people have to skip meals or eat less to make ends meet"—and channeling U.S. funds to international food aid.

"The difficulty we face, though, is that there is so little faith in government and its ability to solve problems. When you serve at a food pantry, you see the person actually receive the can of food you give; it's tangible. But through government there is a disconnect."

BFW provides background on legislation, then asks people to write letters to their congressional representatives or the president. They also encourage phone calls and visits to representatives.

BFW's efforts, along with its lobbying partners on Capitol Hill, including Catholic Charities and the United States Conference of Catholic Bishops, secured a $1.4 billion increase in foreign aid earmarked for poverty relief in the 2007 budget. They also helped to avoid major cuts proposed to food stamps and other hunger-relief programs.

In 2007 BFW is focusing on the Seeds of Change campaign, addressing broad reforms proposed to the Farm Bill, which comes up in Congress every five years for reapproval. Lynch offers a suggested revision to the Farm Bill: "An excess of $3 billion to $5 billion is spent each year to keep farmland from being farmed. We could use that money to buy food to feed the poor. These farmers could grow food specifically for the poor, and the U.S. could buy it and distribute it."

Also on the agenda is passing the Hunger-Free Communities Act, a bipartisan bill that encourages local groups to create a social safety net in their own communities.

Needed: The Political Will of the World

Ending world hunger will take the political will of the world as well as the United States. According to Jeffrey Sachs, economist and founder of Millennium Promise, the question is not "Can rich countries afford to help the poor ones?" but "Can the rich afford not to?" His answer, of course, is no. And while Sachs believes in the fundamental moral obligation to alleviate poverty and hunger around the world, his book *The End of Poverty* appeals even more to the purely economic rationale.

Sachs suggests a five-fold approach for international investment. All five elements must be implemented simulta-

A Famine Unfolds

Stage	Description	Strategies for Survival	Responses	Deaths
Stage One: Food Insecurity	One poor harvest	Reduction of food intake Community emergency supplies Sale of disposable goods	Early warning systems should be in place. Governments and aid agencies should provide resouces that allow people to stay in their villages and continue working.	Less than 1 in 10,000 daily
Stage Two: Food Crisis	Several bad harvests in a row	Sale of items needed for farming Sale of home Killing livestock	Aid agencies and governments should be mobilizing to distribute food aid. Special attention must be given to the very old and very young.	More than 1 person in 10,000 daily
Stage Three: Serious Food Crisis	No harvest	All resources have been used. Dependency on food aid. People leave villages to try to find food.	Food distribution. Medical intervention to stop deaths.	More than 2 in 10,000 daily

continued

A Famine Unfolds [CONTINUED]

Stage	Description	Strategies for Survival	Responses	Deaths
Stage Four: Famine	Failure of government and international community to provide relief. May be caused by conflict. No food.	Strategies have been exhausted. People travel to camps if they are able. Mass starvations. Destruction of community.	Medical intervention. Food relief aid; often must be delivered to people who are too weak to travel.	More than 5 in 10,000 daily

TAKEN FROM: "Lifecycle of a Famine," *Alert.net*, Reuters Foundation, September 15, 2005.

neously to make improvements that last: agriculture, health care, education, infrastructure, and safe drinking water and sanitation.

Under the United Nations Millennium Development Goals, the 22 richest countries in the world pledged to give 0.7 percent of their GNP [Gross National Product] to official development assistance. Similar pledges have been made to the United Nations since 1970. Yet few of these industrialized countries are making good on their promises. In 2005 only five countries met or exceeded a 0.7 percent contribution. The United States gave only 0.22 percent, accounting for almost half of the total assistance shortfall.

Sachs insists that international funds at even 0.5 percent of rich-world GNP would be enough to end extreme poverty in the world. He cites the example of Ghana, which developed a poverty reduction strategy in 2002 that called for $8 billion in foreign aid over five years. Sachs calls the strategy "exceptionally well-designed" with high potential for success. But donors would only come up with $2 billion, and Ghana's attempt at attacking poverty came up woefully short.

Sachs may succeed where others have failed with his ability to popularize the economics of poverty eradication. He's toured Africa on highly publicized trips with superstars Bono and Angelina Jolie, who are happy to lend their names and money to the effort. Students at Columbia University were even selling T-shirts that read "Jeff Sachs is my homeboy."

Small Loans Reap Large Rewards

A major problem for most poor people is that they do not have access to financial services such as lines of credit, savings accounts, or any kind of financial advice or planning. In most of the developing world, bank fees for a simple account are out of reach. As such, cash hidden under a mattress or in a jar is about the only choice.

Often it would take only a very little bit of money (by U.S. standards) to allow poor people to get a leg up on their financial difficulties. A $50 loan could be enough capital to start a fruit stand or a sewing shop. In theory, a person would then be able to support herself sufficiently, as well as pay back the loan over time.

Susy Cheston is senior vice president of Opportunity International, a Christian microfinance organization that serves nearly 1 million clients with small loans. Cheston tells the story of Ana Martinez, a mother of five children in El Salvador. Her family lost everything they had in an earthquake, and Martinez's husband could not find work. They lived in a shantytown in a one-room, corrugated metal house with no plumbing or electricity. But Ana could make beautiful piñatas. She told Cheston, "If I had some paper and materials, I could sell so many of these."

Citizens must contribute to the redefinition of power structures, making steps toward a truer democracy.

So Cheston arranged for a $100 loan, which Martinez used to buy paper, glue, and chicken wire. She quickly increased her business to take in $4 per day, then $6 a day. The first things she did were to enroll her children in school and buy them shoes. A few years later they moved into a three-room concrete home with a roof, electricity, and plumbing.

Well-meaning people often ask Cheston how they can send shoes to the children in El Salvador. "I say to them, 'We certainly could have bought shoes and sent them to Ana, but instead we invested $100 so she was able to buy them herself.' Most importantly she has the pride, dignity, and joy of being able to care for her own children."

When Muhammad Yunus started lending money to poor people, critics said he would never see it repaid. But in fact Yunus found the opposite to be true. From cash loans out of his own pocket, he built the Grameen Bank in Bangladesh, which boasts a 99 percent repayment rate, much higher than that of commercial lenders or credit cards. The recipient of the 2006 Nobel Peace Prize, Grameen Bank now has 6.39 million borrowers, 96 percent of whom are women, and provides services in 69,140 villages.

According to Cheston, only 5 to 10 percent of demand for credit in poor [communities] is met, and savings and insurance are also needed. Out of the 3 billion poorest people in the world, only 10 million have insurance, and a poor person has the highest chance of being a victim to natural disaster, a health problem, or theft. "It's like Chutes and Ladders for them," says Cheston. "Every time they can get a leg up on their finances, they hit one of the chutes of a medical emergency or a robbery. It's a huge setback."

Improving Crop Yields

Another approach to filling empty bellies is to improve yields of local crops, particularly on family farms. Some argue whether large-scale agro-tech programs, such as the famous post-World War II Green Revolution, are successful against hunger, since increased production of food does not necessarily mean that that food is reaching the mouths of the hungry, or even being sold for a profit that benefits the hungry. Furthermore, a heated debate goes on over genetically modified seed varieties.

But most can agree that—especially in areas that have had unsuccessful harvests due to drought, disease, insects, or other pests—heartier seeds, improved fertilization methods, and irrigation can increase food production and help to feed the population.

One success story is the introduction of nitrogen-fixing trees in Sauri, Kenya, a Millennium Promise project. The International Center for Research in Agroforestry introduced a method of planting trees that are able to convert atmospheric nitrogen into a compound that is nutritious to food crops, and is thus a natural substitute for chemical nitrogen fertilizer. As an added benefit, the trees also provide wood for cooking fires.

An Australian institute has developed another way to spread improved agricultural techniques and technology to the developing world using the Internet. Cambia promotes "open source" technology for agriculture, in the same way that software developers share ideas. Much of today's agricultural advancement has been protected by patents that make it expensive or impossible for farmers in the developing world to access it.

Cambia's founder is Richard Johnson, a biotech scientist responsible for developing the primary building block to plant DNA recombination.

"If we're really interested in ending world hunger we have to be focused on what resources are available," says Johnson. "The most important resource is human creativity and commitment to innovate. We are working toward changing options—structurally—in this area."

A Return to a Traditional Diet

In contrast, *Diet for a Small Planet* author Francis Moore Lappe, who credits Catholic social teaching as one of her influences, says that higher agricultural yields are simply not the answer, since there is already enough food to feed the whole planet yet the food is not distributed equally.

The root of the trouble is the centralization of economic power: Those who have power dictate what foods are produced and how they are made available. Those who don't have power are at the mercy of the system. "I came to see how our production system treats even an essential ingredient of life itself—food—as just another commodity, totally divorcing itself from human need," Lappe says.

A prime symptom of this problem, says Lappe, is that nearly half of all grain worldwide is fed to livestock. In the United States it takes an average of 16 pounds of grain fed to cows to produce one pound of beef. Lappe says a meat-centered diet is inherently wasteful, because humans can get protein from plant sources, and Americans already eat twice the amount of protein their bodies can use. In short, wealthier nations create a market demand for meat, so grain gets fed to livestock, and those who cannot afford meat are left without.

Interestingly Lappe is not a vegetarian. "What I advocate is the return to the traditional diet on which our bodies evolved. Traditionally the human diet has centered on plant foods with animal foods playing a supplementary role," she says.

Lappe's daughter, Anna Lappe, has joined the fight for food equality and together they founded the Small Planet Institute. "We know we have persistent hunger because of lack of democracy, not lack of food," says Anna. "People who go hungry have a lack of power over their own food choices. We can shift food democracy by using our own power to choose food from local sources."

Buying Local Food

For those who find choosing locally produced food inconvenient and time-consuming, Anna came out with a cookbook called *GRUB: Ideas for an Urban Organic Kitchen*. Lappe partnered with award-winning chef Bryant Terry, who developed the recipes, from comfort-food macaroni and cheese to "Smoky South American Seitan Stew."

"Every time you spend money on food that has traveled more than 1,000 miles to get to you, you're paying for advertising and marketing of the products," Lappe says. "But when you buy from the farmer, your money goes directly to the farmer."

One way to buy direct from farmers is through community supported agriculture (CSA) cooperatives, in which consumers buy a share in a local farm, which then delivers a portion of its harvest to each shareholder over the growing season. To increase variety and share resources, many CSA groups include several different family farms. Generally the CSA has pick-up points in town centers for weekly or biweekly shipments. Some even offer right-to-your-door delivery.

Beyond a personal diet change, though, citizens must contribute to the redefinition of power structures, making steps toward a truer democracy, Frances Moore Lappe says. Development, too, must be redefined "not merely in terms of more production or consumption, but first and foremost in the changing relationships among people."

Five Ways to Address Hunger

What can you do to end hunger?

- Give a llama, goat, cow, or rabbits through Heifer International for Christmas and birthday gifts, or in honor of a loved one who has passed away (heifer.org).

- Donate to Catholic Relief Services (crs.org), America's Second Harvest (secondharvest.org), or Heifer International.

- Volunteer at your local food bank or serve meals in a homeless shelter.

- Take action through Bread for the World. Call or visit your congressperson and urge him or her to support current legislative priorities (bread.org).

- Give money to a donation-based microfinance institution, such as Opportunity International (opportunity.org), FINCA (villagebanking.org), Grameen Bank (grameenfoundation.org), or Unitus (unitus.org). Catholic Relief Services also has microfinance programs.

European Agriculture and Technology Can Respond to the World Food Crisis

Charles Clover

Charles Clover, the environment editor of the British newspaper, The Daily Telegraph, *reports that there are increasing pressures on world food supplies as well as inflation in food prices. He notes that experts believe that European farmers are responding by growing more food. In addition, making science and technology available to small, developing world farmers will help famine-prone countries to feed themselves. Finally, Clover argues, technologies that will use woody crops for biofuels can help reduce poverty and hunger in Africa, because the continent is able to grow these crops in large quantities.*

As you read, consider the following questions:

1. What percentage of consumer spending goes to food in developing countries, according to Henri Josserand of the Food and Agriculture Organization?

2. According to Clover, in what year will the world population hit nine billion?

3. What are two examples of third-generation biofuels, as noted by Clover?

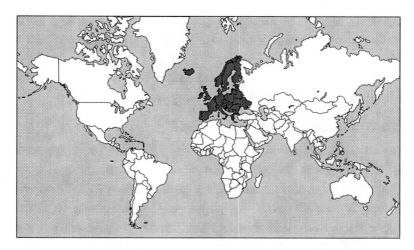

The era of cheap food is over. In Britain, a standard white loaf costs more than £1, grocery bills are driving up inflation and land prices are going through the roof. But steep rises in the price of staples such as wheat and rice are having an even bigger impact on poor countries.

In Cameroon, 24 people have been killed in food riots since February [2008], while in Haiti, protesters chanting, "We're hungry" forced the prime minister to resign this month [April 2008].

The World Food Programme has warned that we could be living in a world of food supply imbalances until 2010 at least.

In the past month, there have been food riots in Egypt, Cote d'Ivoire, Senegal, Burkina Faso, Ethiopia, Indonesia, Bangladesh and Madagascar.

The World Bank now believes that some 33 countries are in danger of being destabilised by food price inflation, while Ban Ki-Moon, the UN [United Nations] secretary-general, said that higher food prices risked wiping out progress towards reducing poverty and could harm global growth and security.

Why has this happened so quickly? Can science and technology get us out of the hole we appear to be in[?]

What Caused the Price Rises?

Bob Watson, the chief scientist at the [British] Department for the Environment, Food and Rural Affairs, puts the rise in the price of commodity crops such as wheat down to a number of factors: higher demand for grain to feed livestock in China, where increasing affluence means more people want to eat meat; drought in Australia for three years, meaning it has had to import wheat; market jitters brought on by the sight of several countries stopping exporting grain; speculators seeing a chance to make money; and, of course, the sudden extra demand for food crops such as maize [corn] for use in biofuels, in both Europe and the United States.

A few years ago, he points out, no one could have predicted that we would be aiming to produce five to 10 per cent of our petrol and diesel from crops.

Since January 2007, the price of wheat has risen by as much as two and a half times, while the rice price has almost trebled.

This, says the International Rice Research Institute, is partly because rice-growing land in countries such as the Philippines is being lost to industrialisation and urbanisation, while the growing appetite for meat and dairy products among Asia's burgeoning middle class is leading farmers to abandon rice growing. Flooding in Indonesia and Bangladesh and cold weather in Vietnam and China have also hit production.

The Poorest Suffer Most

Food price inflation inevitably hits the poor hardest. Food represents about 10 to 20 per cent of consumer spending in the rich world, but as much as 60 to 80 per cent in developing countries, many of which are net food importers, according to Henri Josserand, of the UN Food and Agriculture Organisation.

Bob Zoellick, president of the World Bank, calculates that food inflation could push 100 million people back into poverty, wiping out the gains of a decade of economic growth.

The World Food Programme has warned that we could be living in a world of food supply imbalances until 2010 at least.

The biggest gains [in increasing food production] will come not from new "miracle crops", but from making existing science and technology available to the small-scale farmers responsible for tilling a third of the world's land surface.

What Can Be Done

In the short term, farmers in the developed world are likely to be attracted by high prices and try to grow more staple crops. In Europe, Brussels has abolished set-aside, the practice of paying farmers to leave land fallow, and the signs are that Europe's farmers will grow 13 per cent more cereals this year.

In the developing world, things are less certain, because the poorest in Africa and India have been selling their tools, their animals and the sheets of tin over their heads just to buy food.

For the poorest, recovery is more difficult and aid will be needed. The balance will eventually be restored—nearly half of the world's potential agricultural land is unused.

Technology for Small Farmers

The development of better crop varieties, pesticides and fertilisers has kept the world's food supply growing faster than its population, even though the latter figure is set to hit nine billion by 2050.

British-Kenyan Collaboration Results in a New Technology to Help African Farmers

How Push-Pull Works

Push-Pull is a novel approach in pest management that uses a repellent intercrop and an attractive trap plant. Insect pests are repelled from the food crop and are simultaneously attracted to a trap crop. Maize [corn] is intercropped with a legume, silverleaf desmodium (*Desmodium uncinatum*), and napier grass (*Pennisetum purpureum*) is planted around the intercrop. Both plants provide quality fodder for livestock. Therefore, farmers using Push-Pull technology for pest control not only reap three harvests (maize, napier grass and desmodium), they also dramatically reduce the devastating effects of the parasitic weed *Striga hermonthica* through the effects of desmodium.

Push

Chemicals from desmodium intercrop repel moths

Pull

Chemicals from Napier border rows attract moths to lay eggs

Napier grass   Maize   Desmodium
Maize   Desmodium   Maize   Napier grass

TAKEN FROM: Zeyaur Khan, et.al., "Push-Pull Technology Transforms Small Farms in Kenya," *PAN North America Magazine*, Spring 2008, pp. 20–21. www.push-pull.net.

However, the rate of progress has slowed. According to Dr Watson, who chaired the four-year International Assessment of Agricultural Science and Technology for Development (IAASTD), enormous improvements have been made in productivity, particularly in Asia, but food production in sub-Saharan Africa has decreased. More than 800 million people still go hungry at night and, even in India, where the Green Revolution made some of its biggest strides, some 50 per cent of children in rural areas are malnourished.

To the exasperation of the big agroscience companies, and countries such as the United States, Australia and Canada, the 2,500-page IAASTD report, backed by the World Bank and UN, did not push for big technical fixes.

Biotechnology, in the sense of rapid development of plant varieties, will play a central role in feeding the world this century.

It came down on the side of "multi-functional" agriculture, which incorporates goals such as poverty reduction, water conservation and climate change adaptation alongside conventional efforts to increase production.

It said that the biggest gains will come not from new "miracle crops", but from making existing science and technology available to the small-scale farmers responsible for tilling a third of the world's land surface.

Only by helping them to feed themselves—partly by improving distribution and markets—will the challenges of sustainability, better health and poverty reduction be met.

Where Does That Leave Biotechnology?

Partly in the cold. Biotechnology, in the sense of rapid development of plant varieties, will play a central role in feeding the world this century, says Dr Watson.

But whether transgenic crops and animals—those that have had genes inserted into them—have increased productivity at all is open for debate. Technologies such as high-yielding crops, agrochemicals and mechanisation have mostly helped the better-off.

With the right controls, he says, biotechnology could contribute to greater food production—but he adds that some forms of organic agriculture have a part to play in feeding the poor.

This has led to criticism from the US and other countries, who take a simpler view of GM [genetically modified] crops. Sixty countries have endorsed the report. Britain, typically, has yet to decide.

Good and Bad Biofuels

Watson's lot say using food crops for fuel is environmentally, socially and economically unacceptable. Some would argue that using maize for fuel achieves a 50 per cent reduction in carbon emissions once the fossil fuels used to make them are taken into account.

Others argue that there could be an increase in the greenhouse gases produced, because of the displacement of soya crops from the US into Brazil, where they are grown on land cleared from the forest and where livestock is then displaced on to forest land, which has led to a new peak in its destruction.

Some first-generation biofuels, such as sugar cane, look pretty good, according to Watson. Brazil has some 500 commercial varieties and, arguably, sugar cane does not displace livestock into the rainforest.

Everyone is agreed that the role for science and technology is to bring forward second-generation biofuels—using enzymes to break down cellulose in woody crops such as switchgrass and miscanthus, and farm wastes such as straw.

There are other plans to use plain domestic rubbish. Then there are third-generation biofuels such as algae and bacteria. Watson is pessimistic, believing that it will take five to 15 years for the first second-generation biofuels to become available in sufficient quantities.

In the meantime, Europe and America's targets for including more biofuels in what is sold on the forecourt will place greater pressure on food crops.

Good News

The good news, believe experts such as Richard Murphy, a reader in plant science at Imperial College London, is that fuels made from wastes and woody crops grown on marginal land should eventually beat fuels made from food crops on price.

Cellulose breakdown, he points out, happens on the forest floor every day, thanks to the work of fungi and termites. If we could crack it on a large scale, it would make fuel from waste and woody crops as "cheap as chips"—and the continent capable of growing the largest quantities of woody crops is Africa.

So the solutions to the present crisis may, in the end, help fight poverty and save the planet at the same time.

VIEWPOINT 3

Africa Can Be Saved from Famine Through Genetically Modified Foods

Sunday Tribune (South Africa)

The South African newspaper, the Sunday Tribune, *argues that the inflation in food costs cannot simply be attributed to demand for meat in India and China. Rather, the editorial staff asserts, negative European attitudes toward genetically modified foods is sharply reducing the amount of food available worldwide and is thwarting valuable research. Because there is little evidence against the consumption of genetically modified foods, the newspaper urges Europeans to change their attitudes. By using this technology to increase food production, the gap between supply and demand will close.*

As you read, consider the following questions:

1. What problem do farmers share worldwide, according to the *Sunday Tribune?*
2. In China, what is causing a credit boom, according to the viewpoint?
3. According to the *Sunday Tribune*, what are two ways that genetic science has modified plants?

Sunday Tribune (South Africa), "GM Foods Can Bite at Food Crisis," April 27, 2008, p. 26. © 2008 Sunday Tribune & Independent Online (Pty) Ltd. All rights reserved. Reproduced by permission.

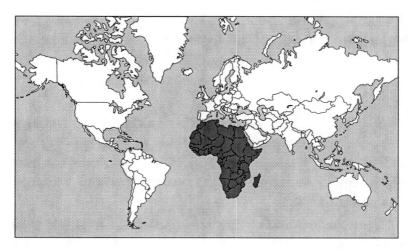

It is remarkable how rapidly the world has moved from worrying about deflation to worrying about inflation; from cheer to despondency about the reduction of poverty; and from concern about food surpluses to panic about shortages.

The hand of rising food prices is suddenly seen everywhere: in the riots in Tibet against Chinese rule; in drastic measures in the Philippines, Egypt, India and many African countries to restrict food exports; in calls for more aid; and even in the Bank of England's reluctance to cut interest rates as fast as its American counterpart.

For agricultural commodity prices (what we call "food") to have more than doubled in the past three years is an astonishing and worrying turn of events.

[F]ood-price inflation is not happening in isolation. If it were, we would be seeing new BMWs popping up in farmyards all over Britain.

A Problem of Our Own Making

But in responding to it, we need to understand the true nature of the problem. And we must recognise that a big part of

197

this problem is our own fault—because of our ill thought-out enthusiasm for using food to fuel cars as well as stomachs; and because of our longer-established but also ill-considered opposition to the use of genetic engineering to help us grow more food.

Start with the true nature of the problem of food-price inflation. Most attention has been given to shortages in supply and to the increased appetite in China and India for meat, which requires more grain. But those explanations are incomplete and misleading.

They are incomplete because food-price inflation is not happening in isolation. If it were, we would be seeing new BMWs popping up in farmyards all over Britain.

Cereal farmers are indeed doing well, but livestock farmers are not, and both share a problem common to farmers worldwide: farming needs fertiliser, and fertiliser needs energy, so farmers' input costs have also risen. Livestock farmers are caught both ways: more expensive fuel and feed for their animals. Rising food prices are directly related to an oil price of $110 a barrel and the inflation in other energy costs, too.

Food Prices Rise with Oil Prices

High demand for energy partly explains those prices. But so, too, does the reluctance of oil-producing countries to expand their output to meet demand. The Opec [an organization of oil producing nations] cartel, spurred on by Venezuela and Iran, does not want its windfall to end, and neither does Russia.

Thus Hugo Chavez [president of Venezuela], supposedly a "Bolivarian Socialist" helping the world's poor, is contributing to a new bout of starvation. If we could get oil supply up and prices down, the food crisis would also fade.

The misleading element of the explanation is the attribution of the boom in food prices to demand for meat in China

Biotechnology Can Increase Food Supply

In many African countries, agriculture is the backbone of the economy employing most of its people and contributing to a major share of its GDP [gross domestic product] and exports. Thus, an improvement in agricultural productivity is vital to ensure the prosperity of its rural sector but also to make food abundant and affordable for all. Biotechnology represents a frontier advance in agricultural science with far-reaching potential in uplifting African food production in an environmentally sustainable manner. Biotechnology represents a powerful tool that we can employ now in concert with many other traditional approaches in increasing food production in the face of diminishing land and water resources.

C.S. Prakash,
"Genetically Modified Crops Are Good for Africa,"
The Vanguard *(Nigeria), February 8, 2005. www.bie.searca.org.*

and India. It is true that, as those countries become more affluent, they are eating more meat. But this is a gradual process.

The immediate issue is that both are suffering from faster inflation, caused by a credit boom. In China, in particular, that credit boom is a result of its efforts to keep its currency artificially cheap. If that policy were to change—as it must, eventually—with a crackdown on domestic inflation, that growth in demand for meat would fade.

In the longer term, it is the self-inflicted wounds we should be addressing. The surge of subsidies for biofuels, which has persuaded many farmers to switch crops, may prove short-lived, but subsidy schemes tend to be difficult to kill off once in place.

The rational approach would be to abandon trade barriers against the cheaper and less-polluting sources of ethanol in Brazil and elsewhere. But rationality and farming policy rarely go together.

Genetically Modified Food Can Solve the Food Crisis

That point can be multiplied a thousand times when it comes to attitudes in Europe to food technology. Every boost in farm productivity has come thanks to technology—from better fertilisers and pesticides to the high-yield rice varieties of India's "green revolution" in the 1960s.

The past decade and a half of scientific discovery has opened up a vista of even greater improvements, yet our reaction has been to reject them all. I refer to genetic science and the ability to modify a plant to make it resistant to pests, to need less fertiliser, as well as many more innovations.

The longer we deny ourselves [genetic modification as a] technological way to increase food output and reduce the use of fertilizer, the longer the current imbalance between food supply and demand will last.

It is sensible to be cautious about science when it comes to our food. But we have rejected GM [genetically modified] foods almost entirely. That rejection has been shared with the European Union [EU], but it cannot be blamed solely on the EU: scares about "Frankenfoods" and the antics of Lord Melchet [former executive director of Greenpeace UK] and Greenpeace [an international environmental organization] are just as responsible.

Europe's unwillingness to accept even a trace of GM products in imported feedstocks forces other countries' farmers to steer clear too. And since the EU is one of the wealthiest regions on the planet, our rejection has set back progress in GM research and development hugely.

This has to change, and urgently. The evidence against genetic modification is as weak as can be. The longer we deny ourselves this technological way to increase food output and reduce the use of fertiliser, the longer the current imbalance between food supply and demand will last.

African Famine Deaths Can Be Prevented Through the Use of New Media

Michelle Hough

World Food Programme writer Michelle Hough reports on a conversation with famine expert Dr. Stephen Devereux who argues that technology and infrastructure improvements have made Asia less vulnerable to famine, although the same cannot be said for Africa. In addition Hough notes, famine deaths can be prevented through the use of media such as cell phones and the Internet. Media can provide early warning of famine and alert relief agencies of conditions within famine areas.

As you read, consider the following questions:

1. Why is food production in Malawi falling, according to Devereux?

2. According to Devereux, why did the possibility of famine in the Balkans in the 1990s attract international attention?

3. How did a refugee get word to the World Food Programme that there was not enough food in the camp where he was staying?

Michelle Hough, "The Changing Face of Famine," The World Food Programme, January 31, 2007. www.wfp.org. World Food Programme © 2008. Reproduced by permission.

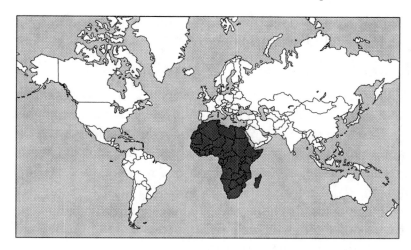

For many of us the face of famine is black, it's poor and it is above all African.

Through the fuzzy focus of the international news machine chronic hunger seems to have a stranglehold on this vast continent, and most of us probably can't remember a time when it was any different. However, do a bit of Googling and you'll find that the top ten worst famines of the twentieth century all took place in Asia.

In a presentation at WFP's [World Food Programme's] Rome headquarters for the book *The New Famines*, Dr Stephen Devereux lays it out clearly in a bar chart: over 30 million people dead in China in 1958, 9 million dead in the Soviet Union in 1921 and over 7 million people killed by famine in the Soviet Union in 1932.

Asia made the move away from famine through improved infrastructure, technology, agriculture and market access, all of which improved food availability.

If you compare the estimated one million who died in the most recent African famine, Ethiopia in 1984, to the large numbers killed in the previous fifty years, there has been a positive change—even though 854 million people around the world are still desperately hungry.

Fewer Famines

"There has been a relative improvement," says Dr Devereux. "Nowadays there are less famines and they affect less people."

Dr Devereux explains that Asia made the move away from famine through improved infrastructure, technology, agriculture and market access, all of which improved food availability.

Democracy also gave people a voice and the power to protect one of their most basic rights: access to food. In India, the post-independence government was made accountable through a social contract outlining the eradication of famine. The country hasn't since experienced famine—although the same can't be said for chronic under-nutrition, which is rife.

African Agriculture and Democracy Have Not Improved

If you look at Africa, says Dr Devereux, not only have factors such as agriculture and democracy not improved, but in some cases there's been a reversal.

For example, food production in Malawi is falling because families with more children have less land to farm. This is exacerbated by the fact that new generations still rely on farming for their livelihoods rather than moving towards new skills.

Victims of hunger can use new media such as the Internet to raise awareness about their condition.

Zimbabwe used to be known as the "bread basket" of its region but now food shortages are frequent.

"In countries such as Zimbabwe and Somalia, poor governance and conflict increase poverty, which increases hunger," says Dr Devereux.

"Meanwhile, in countries such as Ethiopia and Malawi, weak democracy has not strengthened citizens' democratic voices and hunger remains an issue. In Africa, weak democratic processes often exist because minorities take over and exclude the majority," he says.

Another major problem is the dominance of HIV/AIDS in some African countries. Dr Devereux says that AIDS has been a big factor in the resurgence of famine in Africa in the past twenty years because it depletes people's resources and coping mechanisms.

Failure to Respond

In the era of the "new famines", as our potential to eradicate famine increases, so does our potential to cause it, according to Dr Devereux. He thinks that now hunger crises are no longer caused by either food scarcity or market failure, a failure to respond is to blame.

National governments may not be able to protect food security due to conflict or natural disasters. The international community, on the other hand, tends to prioritise some crises rather than others.

"Some famines get international attention, others don't," explains Dr Devereux. "There was a big reaction to the possibility of famine in the Balkans in the 1990s because famine in Europe would have been unacceptable. Iraq got action. Sudan hasn't."

In the "new famine" scenario, the heady mix of national governments, NGOs [non-governmental organizations] and the international community means it's often difficult to lay accountability at the feet of one actor. And besides, no crisis should ever be allowed to get to the emergency stage when fingers are being pointed because it should have been spotted and dealt with earlier, says Dr Devereux.

Using Communication Technology to Address Disaster

"Technology completely alters the way humanitarian work is done," says Caroline Hurford of the World Food Programme (WFP), a United Nations body that is the single largest distributor of food aid. Once upon a time, when disaster struck, big agencies would roll up with grain, blankets and medicine and start handing them out. Victims would struggle to the relief camps, if they could. For aid workers (let alone recipients) there was no easy way to talk to the head office.

Now, when an emergency occurs, the first people on the ground are often computer geeks, setting up telephone networks so other aid agencies can do their stuff. Donors keep track of supplies on spreadsheets and send each other SMS messages: this road has been attacked by bandits, that village cut off by floods. Transport agencies announce helicopter flights by e-mail. Aid providers can find out where exactly on an incoming ship their medical supplies are, saving hours hanging round the docks. Aid donors find it easier to locate the victims of disaster; and victims queue as eagerly for mobile-phone access as they do for food.

Economist,
"Flood, Famine and Mobile Phones: Dealing with Disasters,"
July 28, 2007, p. 61.

Media Is a Major Famine Prevention Tool

"The media is a major famine prevention tool," says Dr Devereux. "It highlights crises that have been concealed and forces people to respond, such as in Malawi in 2002."

He goes one step further and suggests that victims of hunger can use new media such as the Internet to raise awareness about their condition. I tell him that one refugee in a Kenyan camp did exactly that when he sent a text message to WFP in London to say the people in the camp didn't have enough food.

Dr Devereux stresses that the media shouldn't just focus on the powerful images created once famine has firmly taken hold eg. starving children and mass migration.

It should get in there earlier on in the process, when the situation is less "camera friendly" and highlight the numbers affected. It's worth remembering that the effects of malnutrition kill many more people than famine.

WFP tackles hunger before it takes hold with projects such as school feeding and food-for-work which have the dual purpose of providing food assistance while promoting education and training—and in the long-run, providing a brighter future for beneficiaries.

Hopes for the Future

Dr Devereux is hopeful for the future. He thinks the "Right to Food" campaign and other international initiatives will increase and there will be a concerted attempt to prevent famine.

He envisages democracy improving in countries wracked by food insecurity, and biotechnology may offer the potential to increase and stabilise food production. Nevertheless, AIDS will continue to be a big problem, in his opinion.

But, says Dr Devereux, wiping famine from the face of Africa will only be possible if the political will is behind it.

"Our biggest challenge is to move beyond emergencies and have a sustained attack on hunger. We need to make ending global hunger a political priority," says Dr Devereux.

Famine in Asia and Africa Can Be Prevented by Policy Changes

Victor Mallet

Victor Mallet, the Asia editor of the London-based Financial Times, *argues that the 2008 food crisis is not the result of food shortages, but rather is one of poor policy. He offers three solutions for famine prevention. First, governments should not attempt to limit food exports nor hoard food supplies, but should rather allow for free trade. Second, governments should increase food output by helping farmers through easier credit and modern technology. Finally, Mallet asserts, governments must consider policies that will limit population growth.*

As you read, consider the following questions:

1. What has grotesquely distorted international food markets, according to Mallet?
2. What three countries does Mallet cite as having fast-growing populations?
3. According to Mallet, what four natural resources are necessary for food production?

Most of us are used to buying food when we want and it is disconcerting to find that no amount of money will buy you a meal.

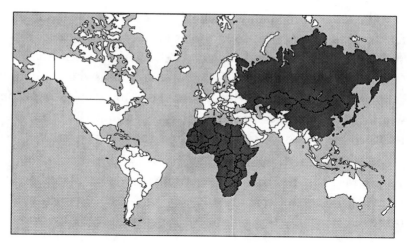

It happened to me once near Quelimane in Mozambique in the 1980s. Even the offer of US dollars in the midst of abject poverty produced only shrugs, because there was simply no food to buy. And it is happening now to the Philippines. Manila has not been able to buy enough rice abroad to secure food for its people, because no one has wanted to sell.

There is thankfully no famine in Manila today. Jollibee, the country's biggest restaurant chain, is offering half-portions of rice and the government has lionised a boxing champion who ate maize instead of rice before his latest victory.

The global food trade on which the populous nations of Asia and Africa particularly depend becomes more dangerously dysfunctional by the day.

The Global Food Trade Is in Trouble

But the global food trade on which the populous nations of Asia and Africa particularly depend becomes more dangerously dysfunctional by the day. The price of rice has more than doubled in a year. Yesterday [April 16, 2008], rice futures hit another record high after Indonesia became the latest producer to restrict exports.

The poor, who spend much of their income on food, suffer the most. Riots over food prices have erupted across Africa and led to the dismissal of Jacques-Edouard Alexis, the Haitian prime minister. Dominique Strauss-Kahn, who heads the International Monetary Fund, says more food price inflation would have "terrible" consequences, including starvation for hundreds of thousands of people and the risk of war.

It is tempting to assume that the problem is purely one of supply and can be fixed by genetically modified plants or investment in a new "green revolution" to boost crop yields. The three most productive solutions, however, are all matters of policy.

Agricultural Trade Must Be Liberalized

First, there is an urgent need for a sustained liberalisation of agricultural trade. The immediate cause of this crisis is not—perhaps surprisingly—a shortage of food. The problem is the sudden reluctance of traditional exporters to sell their surpluses. As with credit providers in the seized-up credit markets, each producer is hoarding its own supply in case of hard times at home, because it suspects its trading partners will do the same. Trust in the efficiency and liquidity of the market has collapsed.

Farm protectionism is not new and international markets are grotesquely distorted by tariffs and subsidies. The main producers—particularly the European Union and the US—have jealously protected their farm sectors from foreign competition, partly on food security grounds.

International farm trade has nevertheless managed satisfactorily for decades to redistribute surpluses of staple foods. The current seizures in the markets are therefore a cause for general alarm. Singapore, one of the world's wealthiest nations, depends on food imports as much as Eritrea, one of the poorest.

Trade Barriers Hurt Everyone

In many countries, governments have imposed protectionist trade barriers, food marketing boards and other arbitrary regulations including heavy tariffs. These have deterred investments that would have increased agricultural output. They have also deterred other forms of entrepreneurship that would have led to economic growth. In Africa, some countries impose tariffs as high as 33 percent on agricultural goods from neighbouring countries, harming farmers and preventing food from getting where it is most needed.

Luther Tweeten,
"Ghana: Famine Amid Plenty,"
Accra Mail, *January 29, 2007.*

The second level at which policies need to change is national. Like international trade, domestic trade in farm produce is often highly distorted. While developed nations tend to support their farmers at the expense of consumers, developing countries typically subsidise city-dwellers at the expense of rural smallholders, who receive low prices and have no incentive to increase their output.

Food Output Must Be Boosted

As the *Financial Times* reported two weeks ago [April 2008], Asian countries are among the worst offenders. Farming productivity growth has slowed drastically in the current decade. "The neglect of agriculture in Asia has got to be corrected," said Ifzal Ali, the Asian Development Bank's chief economist.

Asian governments could do much to boost food output by liberalizing their domestic markets, helping to provide farmers with credit and giving them access to the sort of modern technology and advice they once received as a public service.

Population Control Is Needed

Third and last, governments need to examine their population policies and limit population growth. Although there is enough grain to go round at the moment, you do not need to be a neo-Malthusian [after economist Thomas Malthus, those who believe that limited resources will keep populations in check because those who cannot access food will die] to worry about the demand implications of a global population rising by about 80 [million] people a year or to notice that countries with fast-growing populations—India, the Philippines and Egypt, for example—are especially vulnerable to disruptions in the world's food trade.

Perhaps we should not worry too much that global rice stocks are expected to fall this year to the lowest level in 25 years. Some of the changes recommended above for international and domestic food trade regimes could reverse the decline, probably within a few years.

We should apply some [human] ingenuity to the creation of sound trade, agricultural and population policies, with a view to increasing the supply of food and curbing our demand for it.

A Disturbing Thought

A more disturbing thought is that we may in the longer term be approaching the limits of our ability to exploit the natural resources required for food production—crude oil, cultivable land, soil fertility and available fresh water, to name a few.

Strains on one resource, furthermore, quickly lead to additional strains on another. To make fresh water, more cities are burning fuel to desalinate seawater, but that helps push up the price of oil. To make substitutes for crude oil, farmers are being encouraged to switch to biofuel production, but that uses almost as much fuel as it produces and contributes in its turn to shortages of food.

We must all hope that human ingenuity will foster another green revolution and provide us with the extra food we will need when our numbers top 9 [billion] in the decades to come. In the meantime, we should apply some of that ingenuity to the creation of sound trade, agricultural and population policies, with a view to increasing the supply of food and curbing our demand for it.

Periodical Bibliography

The following articles have been selected to supplement the diverse views presented in this chapter.

Christian Science Monitor	"Market Approach Recasts Often-Hungry Ethiopia as Potential Bread Basket," February 23, 2007.
Delia W. Dugger	"CARE Turns Down Federal Funds for Food Aid," *New York Times*, August 16, 2007.
Economist	"Will It Ever Be Able to Stave off Starvation? Ethiopia," June 14, 2008.
Zeyaur Khan, David Amudavi, and John Picket	"Push-Pull Technology Transforms Small Farms in Kenya," *Pan North America Magazine*, Spring 2008.
Sean Lang	"The Poor Laws and the Irish Famine: Why Did Britain's System of Poor Relief Break Down So Disastrously in Ireland?" *Modern History Review*, vol. 15, no. 4, April 2004.
Colum Lynch	"Aid Agencies Blamed for Current World Food Crisis," *The Sunday Independent* (South Africa), May 25, 2008.
Christine Mikolajuk	"Thanks, But No Thanks: The Other Face of Humanitarian Aid," *Harvard International Review*, vol. 26, no. 4, Winter 2005.
The Nation (Kenya)	"Famine: An Artificial African Problem," February 21, 2006.
New Zealand Herald	"Stopping the World from Starving," April 26, 2008.
Martin Wolf	"The Food Crisis Is a Chance to Reform Global Agriculture," *The Financial Times*, April 30, 2008.

For Further Discussion

Chapter 1

1. In 2008, the world experienced a global food crisis. What were some of the reasons for this crisis, according to the writers of the viewpoints included in this chapter? Which of these reasons seems the most persuasive to you, and after reading the viewpoints carefully, why do you think the world suffered a food crisis in 2008?

2. Many of the writers in this chapter noted that the increasing emphasis on biofuels to provide energy has negatively impacted food supplies throughout the world. What are biofuels and how do they affect food supplies? Make a list of the pros and cons of using biofuels for energy. Should governments regulate the production and use of biofuels to address famine? Or is the potential environmental benefit the most important consideration?

Chapter 2

1. What are some of the climate changes predicted by the writers of this chapter? How will climate change affect the ability of countries to provide adequate food? What responsibility does the world have to poorer nations trying to cope with the consequences of climate change?

2. What are some of the natural disasters cited by the writers of this chapter that can cause or exacerbate famine? Why are natural disasters more devastating with regard to food supply in some countries than in others?

Chapter 3

1. What are some of the ways that political decision making affect famine conditions? How do governments help or hurt their citizens through their actions?

2. What is the role of the World Bank and the International Money Fund in developing countries? Why do some writers argue that international banks have actually caused famine in some places? Are these claims valid?

Chapter 4

1. One response to famine is for relief agencies, governments, and the United Nations to send food aid. Not all would agree that this is the best response. Summarize the opinions of the writers in this chapter concerning food aid and draw your own conclusion to this question: does food aid help or hinder a population recover from famine?

Organizations to Contact

The editors have compiled the following list of organizations concerned with the issues debated in this book. The descriptions are derived from materials provided by the organizations. All have publications or information available for interested readers. The list was compiled on the date of publication of the present volume; the information provided here may change. Readers need to remember that many organizations take several weeks or longer to respond to inquiries.

Action Against Hunger/Action Contre la Faim (ACF)
Action Against Hunger-USA, New York, NY   10018
(212) 967-7800 • fax: (212) 967-5480
e-mail: info@actionagainsthunger.org
Web site: www.actionagainsthunger.org

Action Against Hunger/Action Contre la Faim (ACF) is an international network committed to saving the lives of malnourished children and families while ensuring access to safe water and sustainable solutions to hunger. The ACF Web site includes many excellent resources, including news articles, updates, publications, and links. Sample publications on the Web site include "Prioritizing Local Food Security: Can We Halve Global Hunger by 2015?" and "Action Against Hunger's 2008 Booklet."

Africare
Harold V. Tarver Director, Office of Food for Development
Washington, DC   20001
(202) 462-3614 • fax: (202) 387-1034
e-mail: offd@africare.org
Web site: www.africare.org

Africare is an African American led private, charitable organization dedicated to assisting Africa with such concerns as HIV/AIDS, food security, and agriculture. The Office of Food

Development deals directly with issues of famine and food security. Africare's Web site includes many articles, as well descriptions of programs. Sample articles found on the site include "Africare Food Security Review," "World Food Crisis: Africa's Story," and "Farmers' Innovations."

Bread for the World and Bread for the World Institute
50 F. Street NW Suite 500, Washington, DC   20001
(202) 639-9400 • fax: (202) 639-9401
Web site: www.bread.org

Bread for the World is an international relief agency while Bread for the World Institute is its research and educational partner. The combined Web site has a wealth of materials for any student, including hunger reports, briefing papers, a blog, and links to other anti-hunger organizations. "Recipe for Hope: Responding to the Global Food Crisis" is representative of the articles and brochures available online.

Care
CARE USA, Atlanta, GA   30303
Web site: www.care.org

Care is an international humanitarian organization that identifies as its goal the eradication of poverty around the world. Care provides education, development, and relief assistance to countries in need. The organization's Web site includes many resources, including multimedia and video presentations of its work. Care's annual report describing its work is downloadable from the Web site. On the World Hunger homepage of the Web site, the organization supplies articles such as "The Face of Hunger," "Facts About Hunger," and a "Hunger Quiz."

Center for Global Development (CGD)
1776 Massachusetts Avenue NW, Third Floor
Washington, DC   20036
(202) 416-0700 • fax: (202) 4416-0750
Web site: www.cgdev.org

The Center for Global Development (CGD) is an independent think tank focused on reducing global poverty through policy change in the United States and other developed countries. The organization's Web site includes videos, blogs, links to other resources, and an assortment of other publications. Examples of articles located on the Web site in full text include "Guatemala: Teetering on the Brink?" "How Can We Avoid Another Food Crisis in Niger?" and "Africa Is Given Raw Deal Again."

Christian Reform World Relieve Committee (CRWRC)
3475 Mainway, PO Box 5070 STN LCD 1
Burlington, Ontario   L7R 3Y8
  Canada

The Christian Reform World Relieve Committee (CRWRC) is a church-related relief organization. Their Web site includes many resources, including a PowerPoint show, "World Hunger: Give It Up!" and newsletters from CRWRC field staff in Kenya, Malawi, and Laos. They also include news articles on the Web site such as "Food Distributions Take Place in Haiti," and "Hurricane Ike Strikes."

Church World Service (CWS)
28606 Phillips Street, Elkhart, IN   46515
(574) 264-3102 • fax: (574) 262-0966
e-mail: info@churchworldservice.org
Web site: www.churchworldservice.org

Church World Service (CWS) is a cooperative organization of thirty-five Protestant, Orthodox, and Anglican denominations whose goal is to provide help to those in need, including victims of famine and natural disasters. The group maintains an additional Web site that specifically address problems in Africa and Asia. The CWS Web site includes a video entitled, *CWS: 60 Years of Help and Hope.*

Food, Agriculture and Natural Resources Policy Analysis Network (FANRPAN)

The Secretariat, Pretoria   Private Bag X813, silverton 0127
  South Africa
12 845 9100 • fax: 12 845 9110
e-mail: admin@fanrpan.org
Web site: www.fanrpan.org

Food, Agriculture and Natural Resources Policy Analysis Network (FANRPAN) is an organization that holds as its vision a food secure southern Africa, free from hunger and poverty. The twelve countries of southern Africa are networked through FANRPAN. The Web site provides press releases, links, and publications, including books such as *Silent Hunger: Policy Options for Effective Responses to the Impact of HIV and AIDS* (2007), and *Biotechnology, Agriculture, and Food Security in Southern Africa* (2005).

Food and Agriculture Organization (FAO)

Viale delle Terme de Caracalla, Rome   00153
  Italy
06-57051 • fax: 06-57053152
e-mail: FAO-HQ@fao.org
Web site: www.fao.org

The Food and Agriculture Organization (FAO) is an arm of the United Nations devoted to defeating hunger throughout the world. The organization's Web site is essential for any student studying famine and world hunger. Available on the site are news articles, helpful links, and resources, along with publications relating to the 2008 forum on the global food crisis. Full reports such as *Adapting to Change on our Hungry Planet: FAO at Work 2006–2007* are available for download from the site.

Heifer Project International

1 World Avenue, Little Rock, AR   72202
(800) 422-0474
Web site: www.heifer.org

Heifer Project International is a nonprofit organization that works toward ending world hunger through education and providing livestock to families in need around the world. The organization's Web site includes videos, an interactive map detailing Heifer projects around the world, links to education resources, and full-text issues of *World Ark* magazine.

Oxfam International
Oxfam America, Boston, MA   02114-2206
(617) 482-1211 • fax: (617) 728-2594
e-mail: info@oxfamamerica.org
Web site: www.oxfam.org

Oxfam is an international relief and assistance organization with twelve national offices around the globe. Oxfam's Web site is particularly valuable to students as it has an abundance of articles and resources. Videos, multimedia presentations, up-to-date news articles, links, and photographs document the global situation. Articles like "Oxfam Condemns Lethargic Reaction to Global Food Crisis" and "Ghana: An Activist Works to Protect Her Community" provide a global perspective on issues of food security and famine.

Bibliography of Books

Feargal Brougham, Caroline Farrell, and Brian Malone — *The Great Famine.* London: Evans, 2008.

Marcia Clemmitt — *Global Food Crisis: What's Causing the Rising Prices?* Washington, DC: Congressional Quarterly, 2008.

R.W. Davies and Stephen G. Wheatcroft — *The Years of Hunger: Soviet Agriculture 1931–1933.* London: Palgrave Macmillan, 2004.

Alex de Waal — *Famine That Kills: Darfur, Sudan.* New York: Oxford University Press USA, 2005.

Stephen Devereux — *The New Famines: Why Famines Persist in an Era of Globalization.* London: Routledge, 2007.

Göran Djurfeldt — *The African Food Crisis: Lessons from the Asian Green Revolution.* Cambridge, MA: CABI Publishing, 2005.

Jenny Edkins — *Whose Hunger? Concepts of Famine, Practices of Aid.* Minneapolis, MN: University of Minnesota Press, 2008.

Stephan Haggard — *Famine in North Korea: Markets, Aid, and Reform.* New York: Columbia University Press, 2007.

Stephan Haggard and Noland Marcus — *Hunger and Human Rights: The Politics of Famine in North Korea.* Washington, DC: U.S. Committee for Human Rights in North Korea, 2005.

Leon Hesser — *The Man Who Fed the World: Nobel Peace Prize Laureate Norman Borlaug and His Battle to End World Hunger.* Dallas, TX: Durban House, 2006.

David Keen — *The Benefits of Famine: A Political Economy of Famine & Relief in Southwestern Sudan.* Athens, OH: Ohio University Press, 2008.

Ruth Mayne — *Causing Hunger: An Overview of the Food Crisis in Africa.* Oxford, UK: Oxfam International, 2006.

George McGovern, Bob Dole, and Donald Messer — *Ending Hunger Now.* Minneapolis, MN: Augsburg Fortress Publishers, 2005.

Cormac Ó Gráda — *Ireland's Great Famine: Interdisciplinary Perspectives.* Dublin: University College Dublin Press, 2008.

Raj Patel — *Stuffed and Starved: The Hidden Battle for the World Food System.* Hoboken, NJ: Melville House, 2008.

Richard H. Robbins — *Global Problems and the Culture of Capitalism.* Boston, MA: Pearson/ Allyn & Bacon, 2008.

Paul Roberts — *The End of Food.* Boston, MA: Houghton Mifflin, 2008.

Sharman Apt Russell — *Hunger: An Unnatural History.* New York: Basic Books, 2005.

John D. Shaw   *World Food Security: A History Since 1945.* New York: Palgrave Macmillan, 2007.

Emily Shuckburgh   *The Survival of the Human Race.* New York: Cambridge University Press, 2008.

James Vernon   *Hunger: A Modern History.* Cambridge, MA: Belknap Press, 2007.

Mark Winne   *Closing the Food Gap: Resetting the Table in the Land of Plenty.* Boston, MA: Beacon Press, 2008.

Jean Ziegler   *The Right to Food: Report of the Special Rapporteur on the Right to Food.* Geneva, Switzerland: United Nations, 2005.

Index

Geographic headings and page numbers in **boldface** refer to viewpoints about that country or region.